GOD'S SECRET AGENT

© 2017 by TGS International, a wholly owned subsidiary of Christian Aid Ministries, Berlin, Ohio.

All rights reserved. No part of this book may be used, reproduced, or stored in any retrieval system, in any form or by any means, electronic or mechanical, without written permission from the publisher except for brief quotations embodied in critical articles and reviews.

ISBN: 978-1-947319-01-1

Cover and layout design: Kristi Yoder

Printed in the USA

Published by:
TGS International
P.O. Box 355
Berlin, Ohio 44610 USA
Phone: 330.893.4828
Fax: 330.893.2305
www.tgsinternational.com

TGS001492

GOD'S SECRET AGENT

Diane Yoder

Dedication

To the supreme Author of this story,
who guided my thoughts as I wrote it.
May He receive all the honor and glory.

To Nicu and Monica,
for their faithfulness to our unlimited God.

Table of Contents

	From the Story	ix
1.	A Protecting Hand	11
2.	Through Tears	19
3.	The Good Shepherd	27
4.	The Decision	31
5.	Pastor Liviu	39
6.	"Trust in the Lord"	45
7.	"Not My Will"	53
8.	"In the Army, All Are Soldiers"	59
9.	The Answer	67
10.	A New Era	71
11.	"We Will Not Close This Church"	77
12.	The Inspector's Decision	83
13.	Plans	87
14.	Escape	95
15.	Caught!	103
16.	Where Is God?	109
17.	Together Again	115
18.	The Promise	121
19.	"Please Help Us Bring Our Son"	127

20.	Go or Stay?	133
21.	A New Mission	141
22.	News from Home	147
23.	The Decree	151
24.	The Precious Books	157
25.	The First Trip	163
26.	"God Is a Big God"	169
27.	"God Led Us to This Place"	175
28.	Divine Encounters	181
29.	Priorities	187
30.	Not Alone	195
31.	"All Things Work Together"	201
32.	The Longest Trip	207
33.	God's Secret Agent	213
34.	The Organ	219
35.	"You Must Go Back"	223
36.	The Revolution	227
37.	"I Have No Chance"	235
38.	God Is Not Limited	239
	Afterword	245
	Pronunciation Key	247
	Author's Note	249
	Author's Bio	251

From the Story

Romania, 1988

Pale light shrouded the city of Simeria as Nicu drove toward it. At 5:00 a.m. there were only faint stirrings of life in the streets. He shifted in his seat, forcing his heavy eyes to stay open. He had been driving all night from Germany to Romania. The other three passengers were sleeping, and the large motor home was silent. He longed to rest as well, but he knew he had to keep going and deliver all his goods.

Straightening, Nicu gazed ahead. The city's main street was only a few meters away now. Railroad ties ran across the road, with stones lying between the tracks. Scanning the mostly empty street, Nicu decided to cross the tracks and enter Simeria.

He was halfway across when he realized his mistake. The camper's wheels sank down into the stones between the ties and the axle caught on the track, bringing the vehicle to a dead stop. Try as he might, Nicu could not make it move, forward or backward.

Then it happened.

The first low rumbling sound made Nicu freeze. Within moments the long train was speeding around a distant corner, its whistle blasting. As the deep, mournful sound echoed around him, Nicu punched the pedal in one last desperate effort to move. Nothing.

The train's whistle sounded again. It would soon bear down upon him—and he could not move. So this was it. After all his hard labor to fulfill the calling God had laid on his shoulders, leaving his beloved wife and children at home month after month, it would end like this!

1

A Protecting Hand

He was such a little lad, only six years old, marching into church with his grandmother on Sunday morning. Though no one had told him to do so, he went through every aisle to shake hands with people. *"Pace,"*[1] he would say, returning their greetings. Smiles followed him when he left to sit with the other children. How many little boys came to church with their grandmother before the rest of the family arrived? It was obvious that Nicolae Craiovan loved it.

He had such a good example in his godly *bunica* (grandmother), who often began singing while people were still arriving. His grandfather had been the first Christian in the town of Moldova Nouă, and a minister until his death in 1947. His parents were faithful church members. This little lad came from a good family, strong in their faith. Already he showed promise of following in their footsteps.

Nicu[2] knew that being from a Christian family set him apart from the villagers, who were of the traditional Orthodox faith. "Repentants," they called his people. It was a bad word among Orthodox society, and Christians were often persecuted for their faith.[3] But in their home village of Câmpia, Romania, his parents were well-liked and respected. His mother had a heart

---
[1] Romanian word for "peace." For pronunciation of foreign words, see page 247.
[2] Shortened form of "Nicolae."
[3] The Romanian Orthodox Church is the second-largest of the Eastern Orthodox Christian Churches, the Russian Orthodox Church being larger. Approximately 85% of Romania's people are members by virtue of being baptized into this church as infants. The Orthodox Church practices a ritualistic worship, with icons being an important aspect. In contrast, "Repentants" are evangelical in emphasis, focusing on faith and repentance as well as the baptism of believing adults. Repentants are generally of the Baptist denomination.

for the poor, reaching out to those in need. His father, Petre, stood firmly for what he believed. With five brothers and his sweet *bunica* who lived with them, Nicu was content with his world.

Sunrays slanted through the clouds, reaching to earth with an ethereal glow. The wagon swayed and jolted along the road, pulled by plodding oxen. Nicu sat up straight in his seat, swinging his legs back and forth. Though his *tata* (father) was a mason, he owned portions of farmland outside the village. Nicu liked going along to the fields, where wheat and corn grew tall and golden.

Petre Craiovan strode alongside the wagon, driving the oxen. Nicu's brother Ieremia rode beside him, his brown eyes shining. At eight, he was a year and a half older than Nicu. "Did you see that baby rabbit in the corn? I want to catch one sometime and raise it," he confided.

Nicu grinned. "I'd like to take care of sheep. I saw a boy with his flock today."

"Hey!" Ieremia pointed suddenly. "There goes a rabbit!"

"Where?" Without thinking, Nicu jumped to his feet.

"Watch out!" Tata's shouted warning came too late. As the wagon hit a bump, Nicu's small body catapulted over the side, landing in front of the wagon. There was no time to stop, no time to get out of the way. The wagon's steel wheels rolled directly over Nicu, and when the dust cleared, he was lying still in the middle of the road.

"Nicu!" Tata stopped the oxen and ran toward his son. Kneeling, he lifted him in both arms. "Nicu, can you hear me?"

Nicu's eyes opened slowly. He looked into Tata's scared face, and then at Ieremia, who was hovering over them. "I'm okay," he stated, and the simple words brought tears to Tata's eyes. Nicu looked at him wonderingly. Tata, strong and stoic, seldom cried.

Tata's arms tightened around Nicu. " 'For he shall give his angels charge over thee, to keep thee in all thy ways,' " he quoted, his voice husky with emotion. "The Lord protected you, my son. Hallelujah!"

It was Christmas Day, and holiday cheer filled the air. When Nicu went outside, snow laced the streets and house roofs with intricate patterns. In many lighted windows up and down the street, he could see trees decorated for Christmas. Nicu knew that some families wrapped long candies in foil paper and hung them on the tree. Though there would be no gifts at his house, there would be candy.

They would also have a big Christmas dinner. His mother had been cooking all morning. Earlier that winter they had butchered a pig, and Catarina had divided the meat into jars and heated lard to put into them. The lard would preserve the meat until March, but today they would eat some of it. With mashed potatoes, beans, bread, and cheese, the meal would be a feast.

Nicu's mouth watered just thinking about it. Opening the door, he burst into the kitchen.

Catarina was bending over the stove, her face flushed from the heat. She smiled down at him. "Are you ready to recite a poem for us tonight, Nicu?"

His hazel eyes lit up at his mother's question. On Christmas Eve their family held a church service in their home. He was used to reciting poems; he had recited one the night before in church when the congregation had gathered to celebrate Christmas. Afterward the children had gone out into the streets to sing carols for people. He still had some nuts in his pocket from the treats people had given in return.

"Maybe Nicu would rather sing," said Bunica, her eyes twinkling. She was sitting near the woodstove, holding two-year-old Samuel. "What did you sing when you went caroling last night?"

"We sang 'Silent Night.' " Nicu remembered the way the children's voices rang out in the still, frosty air. "I stood beside Feri."

"Ferdinand, the little German boy?" Bunica smiled. "He's your good friend, isn't he?"

"The boys often play together in the streets," Catarina remarked. "They'll be in the same grade at school."

The door opened, letting in Tata and Ilie with a gust of cold air. *"Brrr!* It's frigid out there," Ilie exclaimed. Taking off his boots, he came to the woodstove. "I thought I was going to freeze while we were milking." Ilie, ten years old, often helped Tata milk the cows. He would leave in another year to attend school in a different village, but that seemed like a long time away.

Tata came to stand beside Mama. "Is the meal ready, Catarina?"

She glanced up with a smile. "Almost." Dishing the mashed potatoes into a bowl, she turned around. "Come, boys, sit down at the table."

Nicu hurried to join Ieremia and Pavel on the bench along the wall. Pavel was four, and Nicu always looked out for him. That was how they did things in their family—the older watched over the younger. Bunica placed Samuel into his high chair and then helped Mama carry the rest of the food to the table. After Tata and Ilie finished washing up, they joined the family.

That evening Tata read the story of Jesus' birth from the Bible. One by one the boys stood against the door, reciting poems and singing. The room became a hallowed place, its sacred beauty folding gently over Nicu.

He lay awake for a long time that night, gazing out the window. The sky was dotted with millions of stars gleaming bright and friendly high above. Maybe this night was like the one when Jesus was born. He heard Bunica singing in the kitchen, "Silent night! Holy night! All is calm, all is bright . . . "

He wished he could have seen the angels who came to the shepherds with the glad tidings of Jesus' birth. He wished he could have seen the wise men who came to Jesus with their gifts. He wished . . . he wished . . .

Nicu jerked awake. The house was dark, but Bunica was still singing, more softly now. "Radiant beams from thy holy face, with the dawn of redeeming grace, Jesus, Lord, at thy birth . . ."

He smiled dreamily. The music made life beautiful.

Nicu sat beside Pavel on the bench behind the table, writing with a pencil. With swift, sure strokes, he wrote his name—N-i-c-o-l-a-e. He was seven now and would soon be going to school, but his mother had already taught him how to spell his name.

Glancing up, Nicu watched Pavel for a moment. Pavel had drawn a house and was now adding trees around it. "Hey, Pavel," Nicu said, scooting closer. "Give me your pencil."

"Why?" Pavel looked up.

"It's bigger than mine. You can have this one." Nicu tossed the pencil he had been using toward Pavel.

Pavel shook his head. "I don't want it."

Nicu straightened. "I'm older than you, so I should have the bigger pencil." His voice held a warning that Pavel chose to ignore. He turned away from Nicu and started wriggling down from the bench.

To Nicu, this was the final straw. Reaching out, he grabbed for the pencil. Pavel resisted and gave his older brother a shove. Losing his balance, Nicu tumbled off the bench. Dimly he heard Pavel shout, but he was already bouncing down the cellar steps nearby. Pain jolted through his body, and everything whirled around him. Then his head struck the cellar floor and everything went black.

At the top of the stairs, Pavel stared down at his older brother in horror. He hadn't realized the cellar steps were so close! What would Mama say when she found out? He must hide!

When Catarina found her son in the cellar, he was moaning. Blood stained the floor around his head. She cried out and rushed to his side, lifting him carefully in her arms. Then they raced to the doctor.

"This could have been bad," the doctor said after he examined the small boy. "He's hurt on the front and back of his head, but it won't affect his brain." He shook his head.

"The Lord protected him," Catarina said, her voice trembling.

"Well, a protecting hand is definitely over him," the doctor said as he dismissed them.

Nicu held Mama's hand tightly as they went out the door. He still felt light-headed and weak, but the doctor's words had sent his spirit soaring. The Lord was watching over him!

Bible in hand, Nicu approached the church doors. The morning service was over, and he was eager to go outside with his friends. He felt especially excited—he had been asked to sing a solo in the choir in a couple weeks. He wasn't afraid, for he loved singing.

"Nicu?" The gentle voice made him turn. Ani stood behind him, smiling. Christina stood beside her, watching him with kind eyes. Nicu liked these ladies who'd arranged a choir and orchestra for the children. Both were single, and people said they didn't want to get married, but only work for the Lord.

Nicu hesitated. What did they want with him?

"Can you stay here a moment?" Christina asked. "We want to talk with you and your parents." With that, she walked over to Nicu's parents.

Nicu saw the questioning looks on his parents' faces as Christina talked with them. Then they both smiled and came toward him with Christina. "Why don't we go into the room where we practice singing with the children?" Ani suggested, turning to lead the way.

Still wondering what was happening, Nicu followed the others into the room. Closing the door, Christina spoke softly to him. "Ani and I have seen how active you are in the church, Nicu. We want to pray that you will preach the Gospel further."

His eyes widened. Preach the Gospel? He was only eight years old! But he knelt obediently on the floor, putting his hands together and closing his eyes. Christina prayed first, and then Ani, asking God to bless Nicu and lead him to become a missionary.

When Nicu looked up, both ladies were smiling at him. There were tears in Mama's eyes, and Tata was holding out his hand. "Come," he said, his hand closing lovingly over Nicu's small one. "It's time to go now."

Nicu was quiet on the walk home. What had he done that stood out to Ani and Christina? He loved going to church and liked participating in church activities, but he hadn't known anyone was watching.

Birds sang in the trees. The sun shone brilliantly. The words that Christina and Ani had prayed gave Nicu an inner strength and joy whenever he thought of them. This was a powerful event in his life; it had happened just for him and none of the other children. Was it truly possible that he would someday preach the Gospel? Be a missionary?

Home was coming into sight ahead. Dismissing his thoughts, Nicu raced his brothers to the gate. There would be time to ponder these things later.

2

Through Tears

"Petre, it doesn't work the same way anymore. You have to give in."

The official spoke with authority, his posture stiff and straight. Nicu looked from the official to his father, who was standing impassively beside him. What would happen next?

All around them people had been joining the collective farm as the Communists took over their land. Some ran into the woods to hide rather than sign the paper that forced them to give up their land. Others committed suicide rather than sinking into poverty.

Petre did not want to join the collective farm. His own land provided well for their family. With the cows' milk they could make cheese, butter, and cream. In the cellar they kept potatoes, vegetables, and cornmeal. They had land outside the village to grow crops. They raised pigs, goats, sheep, and chickens. Ducks and geese completed their little farm. All this would be taken away if he gave in.

But now, Petre Craiovan knew he had no choice. With a trembling hand he took the pen to sign, and tears came to Nicu's eyes. Tata was the last one in the village to give up his freedom. It was 1960.

The official was soon gone, leaving a heavy sadness hanging over the family. As the days passed and the animals were taken away, anger began mixing with the pain in Nicu's heart. *Why did the Communists do this?* All but one of their seven cows were taken, and now they seldom drank delicious warm milk because it had to be saved for cheese. They could do no gardening; there was only a small piece of land outside the village to farm.

"Nicu, please read Romans 8:28 from the Bible," Catarina said one morning. She stood at the stove, cooking cornmeal and eggs. She worked almost mechanically, the sparkle in her eyes gone.

Nicu turned the pages carefully. Mama often asked him to read aloud from the Bible when she was working in the kitchen. On Sundays she fasted all day, praying for Tata, her children, and the church. On those days she would ask Nicu to taste the food to determine if it needed more salt. "He's the girl in the house," Mama sometimes laughed in reference to Nicu's discerning palate. But there was little laughter these days. How Nicu longed to see his mother's eyes sparkle again!

"And we know that all things work together for good to them that love God, to them who are the called according to his purpose," Nicu read slowly. He glanced up. Mama brushed away a tear and stirred the cornmeal a few minutes longer.

"All things," she said softly at length. "That's what God promises. All things."

Weeks passed, and life for the Craiovans settled into a new normal. Nicu's parents accepted the change. Bunica's peaceful voice did not falter when she said, "The Lord has promised never to leave or forsake us." Nicu didn't doubt it. His parents and grandmother took the Bible literally, and in this they found life-sustaining joy.

"Are you boys ready for church?"

Mama's call was usually enough to spur Nicu into action, but now he made no answer. Slowly he put down his comb, a frown furrowing his brow.

"Nicu?" His brother Samuel nudged him. "You had better hurry." Then he looked closer at Nicu's face. "Is something wrong?"

"I'll get a bad mark in school for going to church today." Nicu's voice was so quiet that Samuel had to lean forward to hear. "All the students are supposed to go to school on Sundays, you know. From there the teachers take them to a concert. Whoever doesn't go gets punished."

"They only do that so we can't go to church."

"I know. But sometimes I get tired of being treated differently." There was pain in Nicu's eyes as he turned to his brother. "They look down on us just because—"

"Boys!" Mama's call came again, more urgent this time.

Nicu straightened his shoulders. "Coming," he called back. He was always ready to go to church. That hadn't changed in spite of the ridicule he faced at school. He was in fourth grade now, and each year found him at the top of his class. Though he made friends easily, being from a Repentant family set him apart.

The forested hillsides, cloaked in autumn russets and golds, shook off Nicu's melancholy as he walked down the street toward church with his family. He didn't care too much about the pressures at school when he could look forward to a wonderful time at church. His steps quickened. There would be singing and good preaching, and he would stand up front to recite a poem from memory.

He enjoyed the church service that day, but the world at school was always there to cast a shadow over Nicu's life. Christmas was another season that the school celebrated differently from the church. Teachers spent time teaching their students poems and songs for a Christmas program that celebrated communism, and the children decorated the hall with pine branches and streamers made from colored paper. Many people gathered in the village hall on the appointed evening, filling a vast area of seats.

"Are you ready for tonight?" Nicu asked Feri as they waited with the other children behind the curtain.

"I think so." Feri glanced toward the curtain and took a deep breath.

"What are you scared of?" Nicu asked nonchalantly. "Reciting poems is easy."

Feri shot him a look. "Maybe for you, but not for me!"

Nicu grinned. With a red necktie, white shirt, and dark pants, he and Feri were dressed like all the other boys around them. The colors of their outfits symbolized communism. The girls also wore red ties, white blouses, and dark blue skirts. But all this made no difference to Nicu. He had a plan.

The curtain was lifting. It was time for the program to start.

Nicu filed out with the others. When they saw the overcrowded hall, some of the children began crying and darted back behind the curtain without giving their pieces. But Nicu, accustomed to reciting poems before big crowds in church, wasn't afraid. He stood calmly, waiting his turn.

At last it was time. Stepping to the front of the platform, Nicu straightened, standing erect. His wavy brown hair shone in the fluorescent lighting as he looked up toward the ceiling and began reciting:

> Jesus, you came into the world
> O holy and divine child,
> To take away the sins
> That prevail on earth.

Gasps came from the audience. What was this little boy doing?

> You came, but not in glory;
> You were born in a humble manger.
> This was the will of the heavenly Father;
> Peace and goodwill to men you brought.
>
> You healed the sick,
> Blind, and crippled.
> Yet the treacherous, evil world
> Would ask that you die.

Nicu's voice rang out, clear and strong. There was no sound from the audience. Moving his gaze from the ceiling to the crowd in front of him, he made a sweeping gesture with his hands toward the audience.

> But, oh evil world, you know
> That He will come again;
> Not for salvation,
> But for judgment.
>
> And then, when you stand in front
> Of Him whom you have crucified,
> What will you answer
> When He says, "I do not know you"?[4]

Nicu paused, his eyes scanning the crowd. His parents and his *bunica*, sitting near the back of the room, had heard him recite the poem last Sunday night in church. He knew they would not chide him for reciting it again that night.

There was one thing left to do. Nicu bowed and walked behind the curtain.

Everyone clapped.

While most of Nicu's teachers never degraded him for what he had done at their Christmas program, he quickly discovered that Miss Mariana would. The fifth-grade teacher who taught the Russian language class was a staunch Communist who came from the southern part of Romania where the president lived. At twenty-seven, she was unmarried and had just finished college. She kept order in her classroom with a stern hand.

Nicu shifted his position on the bench. Invigorating breezes drifted

---

[4] Author unknown.

through the open window, inviting him outside. But only after school was dismissed would he be free to play football with his brothers and friends in the street. Right now he had to study for a test.

"Repentant!" The strident hiss in his ear jerked Nicu from his studying. As he looked up, something flashed in his teacher's hand, and the pointed tip of a spindle punched his ear. Nicu's hand flew upward and came away sticky with blood. He stared after Miss Mariana as she stalked away. A hush fell over the classroom as the other students watched in stunned silence.

Nicu bowed his head, tears starting to his eyes from the pain in his ear. But there was an even deeper pain in his heart. Being from a Christian family had always set him apart from the other students. Some didn't want to be friends with him, and it was common for the teachers to give him lower grades than he deserved. Now this had happened. But there was nothing he could do to change his circumstances. The teachers had high authority over the children, and he could get a bad mark if he reported it.

Nicu managed to shake off the bad memory for a while that evening as he played football with his brothers and friends. But he slipped in early to be with Mama in the kitchen as she cooked supper. When she asked him to read once again from the Bible, Nicu hurried to where the book lay on the shelf. He lifted it reverently and carried it back to his chair.

"Why don't you read from Matthew 5:10-12 tonight?" Catarina asked. She salted the bean soup and turned to look at him through the rising steam.

After a few moments Nicu had found the passage. "Blessed are they which are persecuted for righteousness' sake: for theirs is the kingdom of heaven." He hesitated.

"Go on," Mama encouraged.

"Blessed are ye, when men shall revile you, and persecute you, and shall say all manner of evil against you falsely, for my sake. Rejoice, and be exceeding glad: for great is your reward in heaven: for so persecuted they the prophets which were before you."

Glancing up, Nicu met his mother's kind gaze. "Oh, Mama," he whispered, tears coming again to his eyes.

Mama placed a hand on his shoulder. "Never forget this, my son. When others treat us wrongly, it is for Jesus' sake. We have nothing to be ashamed of."

Nicu watched as she turned back to her work. The Bible, still open on his knees, felt warm and comforting.

3

The Good Shepherd

The Sunday evening service was over, and young people were crowding around the entrance doors. Thirteen-year-old Nicu dodged around a huddle of older boys, trying to keep up with his friends who were hurrying down the steps. He stopped short when one of the older boys caught his arm. "Hey, Nicu, there's something you should see," Gheorghe said, lowering his voice conspiratorially.

"What's that?"

Gheorghe winked. "Come along with us to the cinema, and you'll see."

Nicu stared. Gheorghe was at least seventeen—five years older than he—and knew as well as he did that the church did not allow them to go to movies. Besides, his parents would never allow it. Why was Gheorghe inviting him to go along?

"We're heading over there right now." Gheorghe's voice sounded warm and friendly. "It'll be lots of fun! Just don't tell your parents. They'll never find out you were there."

Shaking his head, Nicu started to turn away. A mocking voice stopped him. "What? Are you scared?" The other boys snickered.

That did it. He was not going to let these boys call him a coward!

But Nicu did not enjoy the movie at the village hall. The two hours were torture. He stood shaking at the window, afraid his parents would come and find him there. When at last the lights came on, his worst fears were realized. There was Tata, standing outside!

Nicu didn't wait for the other boys. His heart sinking, he went out into the darkness. Tata was waiting for him, tall and stern and sad. He asked only one question: "Why did you do this?"

As they walked home through the night, Tata said, "You are young, Nicu, but those boys know you are already thought highly of at church. They wanted you along so that if they were caught, they could point at you and say, 'He was there too.'"

Nicu hung his head. He knew it was going to take time to rebuild the confidence that people had had in him.

"Your mother put food on the table for you and went to bed," Tata went on. "She was crying."

Nicu fought back tears of his own. "I can't eat, Tata. I'll never do this again—I promise."

He renewed that promise in his heart the next day when Mama took him aside and prayed with him. His parents were doing their best to train him in the way he should go, and he was determined never to part from it again.

"Hey, Nicu!"

Nicu, swept out the school doors by a jostling crowd of students, glanced back. His friend Feri broke into a jog and caught up with him outside. "Are you going straight home?"

"I have to take the lambs out to the pasture, so I should get home right away. What's up?"

"I thought maybe we could play football or something, but I guess you have other things to do." The boys turned onto their home street. The weather was turning cool as the early school days slipped toward autumn. "I like school pretty well this year," Feri confided.

"I like it too. I chose to go to French class right away, rather than go back to Russian—and I have a good teacher."

"At least this one doesn't punch your ear with a spindle tip." Feri's eyes narrowed.

Nicu shrugged, not wanting to think about it anymore. "Here's my gate. I'll see you later, Feri."

"Bye." Feri waved as Nicu opened the gate. For a moment he stood still, watching Feri continue down the street. The German boy was a good friend.

Closing the gate again, he slipped into the house. His mother was in the kitchen, slicing bread and cheese. "There you are," she said, looking up with a smile. "I saw you walking with Feri."

"We always walk home together." Nicu set his lunch pail on the counter. "I wish I could spend time with him in the evenings, though."

"Once winter comes, you'll have more time," Catarina said. "You won't have to go out with the lambs as much. Here, I packed a little bread and cheese for you to take along to the pasture."

"Thanks, Mama." Nicu took the brown paper sack and hurried out the door to the barn. The lambs in their stall bleated for joy when they saw him coming.

Nicu led the flock out to the pasture. Rolling hills spread out under the azure sky, dappled with fleecy white clouds. Distant mountains rose tall and majestic, and the wind ruffled through flower-brocaded grasses at his bare feet. He sank down into the soft grass and opened the paper sack his mother had given him, letting the lambs frisk and graze around him.

As he watched the lambs, Nicu's thoughts roamed. It was hard to believe that in a few months he would celebrate his fourteenth birthday. He was getting older and didn't have long to be at home anymore. Nicu knew that when he turned fourteen he would be sent to boarding school for more education. It was what his father wanted. "I don't want you to follow me in this job as a mason, son," Petre would say. "Building with stones, cement, and brick is heavy, difficult work, and you aren't that robust. I want you to go to school."

Nicu liked watching Tata work and wished he could do it himself. But what Tata said was the final word on the subject. He didn't mind, though. All the other young people in the village had to go to school too. Tata wanted him to attend high school, but it cost too much. The boarding school's price wasn't as high.

Crumpling up the now-empty paper sack, Nicu stretched out in the grass. He stroked a lamb's thick woolen coat as it wandered by. Other lambs drifted close, then farther away as they searched for grass. Nicu rolled over onto his back. The sun touched his face, its warmth making him drowsy. The peaceful setting quieted his thoughts, lulling him to sleep.

Nicu awoke with a start. A hand was shaking his shoulder. He looked up to see a man from the village standing over him. "You must have been deep in dreamland," the man chuckled.

"Where am I?" Nicu rubbed his eyes and looked around, still only half-aware of his surroundings. The sun was sinking toward the west, throwing long, cool shadows across the hills. How long had he slept?

Then a sudden thought struck him, and he sat up straight. "Where are my lambs?"

"They're here," the man assured him, still chuckling. "You must be a good shepherd if they didn't wander off while you slept!"

Then Nicu saw it—the flock of lambs all around him, still frisking and grazing as they had before he had fallen asleep. *A good shepherd,* the village man had said. It reminded him of what the pastor had preached in church recently. "If you're a good shepherd, the sheep will stay around you. Jesus is our Shepherd, and we want to follow Him." Unlike him, Nicu knew, the Good Shepherd never slept, but always watched over His flock. "I know my sheep, and am known of mine," the pastor had quoted. "I lay down my life for the sheep." Nicu knew that such a Shepherd would keep His flock forever.

Standing up, Nicu called to his lambs and led them homeward.

4

The Decision

How Catarina's mother-heart ached to see her son ready to leave for boarding school! He was still so young, only fourteen years old. His height was shorter than average, and that made him seem even younger. But his eyes were clear and steady, and the boyish lines in his face spoke of innocence and purity. Catarina had to wonder if her son would be true to what he had been taught, and if the light in his eyes would remain unclouded in the onslaught of pressures and temptations he would face in the next four years of his life. She could only pray to that end.

On the morning Nicu was to leave, the family had already gathered to pray for him. Now Catarina looked at her son. "Nicu, from now on my eyes will not see you—what you'll do, what you'll speak, or where you'll go. But don't forget, God's eyes will see you anytime and all over." She spread out her hands. "My hands are clean because I gave everything I could for you to follow Jesus. I have done my best."

Nicu looked back at her solemnly.

"I see your growth and the talents in you," Petre was saying to Nicu. Catarina brushed a hand across her eyes and focused on her husband. "I can see in you a gift for becoming a leader in the church. But in the church there will always be problems. Don't forget—the dogs are barking, but the bear controls the road. The bear keeps a straight line and isn't distracted by the barking dogs." His voice grew a little husky. "Keep your eyes on Jesus, son, and don't worry about what others are doing. The water is always moving, but the stones stay where they are at."

The boarding school was in Timişoara, a city 150 kilometers[5] away from Câmpia. Though he planned to travel home for vacation every three months, Nicu's parents knew their son would be basically on his own. Hard as it was, they would have to let him go and trust the Lord to watch over him.

"And so, what we see today comes from the great explosion that created the world millions of years ago."

The teacher's voice droned on, but Nicu wasn't listening anymore. Folding his arms, he looked around the room. Timişoara's boarding school was a big place, with more than three hundred boys attending. The building was several stories high and surrounded by a high barbwire fence. The schedule required the boys to wake up by 5:00 in the morning and exercise until breakfast. School started at 8:00. Sometimes the high walls and rigid schedule felt like a prison.

It hadn't taken long for Nicu to realize that he was the only Christian in his class. But his outgoing nature had quickly won him friends. He had been glad to find a church where he could receive spiritual nourishment through preaching and the fellowship of other believers. As his friendships grew, he had learned to trust three of the church brethren as his mentors.

Nicu jerked back to the present. The dismissal bell was ringing, and the teacher was saying, "Class is dismissed."

Standing up quickly, Nicu gathered his books. He glanced toward the front of the room. The teacher was vanishing through the door, leaving the boys still milling about. Nicu seized the moment. "Do you actually

---

[5] About 93 miles. 1 kilometer = 0.62 mile.

believe all they're teaching us?" he asked Costel, who was gathering his own books nearby.

Costel straightened and shot him a puzzled look. "Why wouldn't I?"

"It goes totally against what the Bible teaches."

"The Bible?" Costel raised his eyebrows. "How do you know the world wasn't created with a big explosion?"

"The Bible says God created the world," Nicu answered.

"Where?" Costel still looked skeptical.

"In the very first verse." Though he didn't have his Bible, Nicu knew the verse by heart. The Scriptures he had read in the kitchen during his childhood came back to him now. " 'In the beginning God created the heaven and the earth,' " he quoted. "God created the first people in the world, Adam and Eve. He put them in the Garden of Eden, but then they sinned and He drove them out. Many years later He sent His Son Jesus Christ to earth."

"Wait a minute." Iosif was standing with them now. "How do you know Jesus Christ actually existed?"

"John 3:16 says, 'For God so loved the world, that he gave his only begotten Son, that whosoever believeth in him should not perish, but have everlasting life.' That Son is Jesus Christ," Nicu declared.

"You have no proof of it," Iosif said scornfully.

"Oh, but I do! The Scriptures speak of how Jesus was born in a manger." Impulsively, Nicu jumped up on the nearby bench. "We always celebrate His birth at Christmas!"

As his voice rose, the other boys turned to watch. Nicu was still talking, trying to convince Iosif. "The angels came to the shepherds and brought them the good tidings. Wise men traveled very far to bring gifts to Jesus. I tell you, there is indeed a Jesus Christ!"

"Preach it, Nicu!" someone called out. A wave of laughter swept through the room.

Nicu refused to back down. "All of you need to know this," he addressed the growing crowd. "Jesus loves us so much that He died on a cross for our sins and rose again in three days to give us eternal life."

"He wouldn't have needed to bother!" another boy shouted. Hoots, whistles, and cheers met this clever comment.

Nicu hesitated, looking at the boys. They were growing excited, and in a crowd this size, anything could happen. They were all against him, and he wasn't getting anywhere. He slowly stepped down from the bench, a heavy feeling settling over his heart. Why had he ever done this? It was fine to speak to groups of people in church, but this was different. This was school, where classmates could turn against each other. It would have been better to speak to each one privately.

Picking up his books, he headed toward the door. His German friend Robert caught up with him there, a smile playing around his lips. "I like your enthusiasm, Nicu," he said. "You just need to be careful where you talk about things like that."

"I know it now, Robert," Nicu said ruefully. "Do you think it'll make any problems?"

Robert shook his head. "You're a good friend to everyone. After all, who else helps us with our schoolwork?"

Nicu grinned a little. From his seat on the back bench in the classroom, he listened well and often took notes in class. Sometimes he passed them forward under the benches to help others.

"That's a good friend, all right," Robert chuckled. "Seriously, though, the boys respect you. They know what you believe and where you stand."

Nicu was silent. He appreciated his friend's words, but he knew one thing—he wouldn't be doing this again.

After this spontaneous preaching outburst, he felt marginalized. The desire for friends began to outweigh his desire to proclaim his faith, and he determined to be a quieter Christian. Certainly God would understand his desires, would He not?

And so, gradually, Nicu allowed the spiritual disciplines that used to mean so much to him slip away until they were no longer a priority in his life.

The table was spread with one of Mama's delicious meals—cooked cornmeal, fried eggs, bread, and cheese. Tata led in prayer, thanking God for bringing their boys home safely once again and allowing them to be together as a family. Hearing the emotion in his voice, Nicu brushed a hand across his eyes.

Since leaving for boarding school, some of his best memories were from the times he had come home for vacation. But this time was different. A cloud seemed to hang over the days that should have been filled with sunshine. If his dear mother sitting across from him would know what had been happening to him in recent months, it would hurt her. And Bunica, her face aged and wrinkled, watching her grandsons with that quiet gleam in her eyes—what would she say?

His parents found a chance to talk alone with him that afternoon in the kitchen. "How are your studies going?" Tata asked.

"Very well." Nicu leaned back in his chair. "I've never had any trouble in my work."

"Do you still attend church? Here, I made you some tea." Catarina handed him the tea cup and sat down beside Tata.

"Thanks, Mama. Yes, I attend church," he added. He decided, however, not to mention his waning attendance. "There's also a famous evangelist who often comes into the college dorms to pray with us. Lots of young people get saved through Liviu Olah's preaching."

Tata's eyes seemed to look straight into his heart. "How is your relationship with the Lord, son?"

Nicu shifted uneasily in his chair. He took another sip of tea. The ticking of the clock sounded loud in his ears. *Don't forget, God's eyes will see you anytime and all over . . .* His mother's words seemed to echo in the stillness. How often those words had come to his mind in the past years when he had faced temptations! How could he tell them the truth?

"My life has been a little uncertain lately," he said carefully, searching for words. "Things haven't been going so well, and I—" He stopped short as he saw the pain in his mother's eyes. "Please pray for me," he finished quietly.

Soft and low her answer came, falling like soothing balm on his troubled heart. "We've never stopped praying for you, son."

A rain shower earlier that day had washed the earth fresh and clean. Raindrops still clung to the grass along the road, and trees were beginning to bud in early spring. But Nicu barely noticed the beauty of the March evening as he hurried down the street.

Glancing ahead, he saw the church he was attending in Timișoara. He had bribed the watchman into letting him go without reporting him, and looked forward to spending time with other believers. But now as he looked at the building that held up to eight hundred people, Nicu's steps slowed. He knew that he would soon have to make a decision—either give Christ his whole heart or turn from what he had been taught all his life and live for his own pleasure. What did he really want?

Walking slowly on, Nicu went up the steps into the church. The choir was already singing, their voices resounding throughout the room. "Amazing grace! How sweet the sound that saved a wretch like me! I once was lost, but now am found; was blind, but now I see . . ."

Was it a message for him? Nicu pondered the words as the choir continued to sing. When at last the pastor rose to preach, he straightened in his seat.

Pastor Liviu Olah's message spoke of the glories of heaven and the horrors of hell. "Turn with me in your Bibles to Matthew 24," he said. "Verse

35 says, 'Heaven and earth shall pass away, but my words shall not pass away.' There is darkness on the earth under the rule of Satan. For those who will not believe in the Lord Jesus Christ, there is the fear of hell, which is eternal suffering."

Toward the end of his sermon, Pastor Liviu spoke about heaven. "The angels live in heaven, and those who believe in the Lord Jesus Christ will also live there. How wonderful is the Lamb who takes away all our sins! He will reign in heaven for eternity." Closing his Bible, he looked out over the crowd. "Do you believe that Jesus Christ is the Son of God? Do you believe that He can be your Savior right now and right here?"

Nicu bowed his head, tears coming to his eyes. The burden of sin on his heart was so great that he couldn't stay in his seat a minute longer. Raising his hand, he went forward to the front of the church. As he knelt to pray, the audience seemed to fade away and he was alone with God, repenting from his sins with brokenness of spirit.

Pastor Liviu prayed for all those who had responded. When at last he rose from his knees, Nicu's face was shining with the light of God's love. The blood of Jesus had washed his soul clean and filled his heart with the Holy Spirit.

The pastor met with him after church. "God bless you for answering His call on your life, Nicu. Conviction is one of His greatest gifts, and if we respond to it, God is able to use us for His glory." His clasp was warm and strong as he shook Nicu's hand. "You're welcome to join instruction class," he went on, smiling. "We'll be meeting once a week for a couple of months before the baptism."

"Thank you, pastor. I have to get a pass whenever I leave boarding school, so I may not always be able to come. But I'll be there as often as I can."

As he descended the church steps, Nicu marveled at the peace he felt deep within. The message had brought a revival to his heart, and he knew that this was a turning point in his life.

Pastor Liviu Olah sat in his office, writing down the names of the young people he planned to baptize on October 20, 1968. There were twenty in all, with Nicolae Craiovan as the youngest. The Romanian Communist Party required a list of the people whom pastors baptized. Eighteen was the required age for baptism, and the applicants were to be from a Christian family.

All the people on this list were either eighteen years old or above—except Nicu. He would not have his birthday until December. Liviu's brow furrowed. Pastors didn't dare baptize young people before they were eighteen, but he was determined to make an exception this time. The young man hadn't always been able to attend the classes, but he was active in the church. Often he recited poems and Bible verses from memory, and he willingly helped with missionary work in the villages surrounding Timişoara. "I'm going to baptize this one!" Liviu declared aloud in the stillness of the room.

Baptismal morning dawned clear and bright, with a turquoise sky and autumn-cloaked trees. Nicu's voice carried clearly over the full church from where he stood in water at the front to recite a poem.

> My life is full of you, Lord;
> With everything I worship you.
> Near to your divine cross
> I kneel and thank you . . .

When he had finished the recitation, Nicu knelt in the water. As Pastor Liviu Olah baptized him, joy filled his heart. He had made his decision, and there was no turning back.

5

Pastor Liviu

Darkness shrouded the hulking shape of the boarding school. A silver moon hung low in the sky, its pale light catching signs of activity near the window at the corner on the second floor. A cluster of boys surrounded it, watching the lithe figure descend the wall to the ground. The young man hit the ground running and didn't stop until he reached the road. Pausing, he looked back. His classmates had already closed the window, but he knew they would open it again when he ascended the wall upon his return.

Setting a rapid pace, Nicu hurried down the street. Stars shone high above, and night creatures filled the air with their music. The church service started at 6:00, but he hadn't been able to receive a pass to leave the school's campus. Undaunted, he had decided to sneak out through the bathroom window and attend.

When Nicu strode into the entry, he found Pastor Liviu stepping out of the pastor's office. "Peace be with you, young man," he said, reaching out to shake Nicu's hand. "How are things going?"

Nicu smiled. "Very well, pastor." Now in his fourth year of boarding school, he had recently started working at a factory as an engineer. It was a part of the school's system—one day of the week was school, and the other days he worked in the factory, practicing what he was learning. "God has been good to me."

"Do you have a word to share for Him?" Liviu asked.

"I took some notes in my personal devotions this morning," Nicu said quietly. "I was reading in Matthew 24, and it really spoke to me."

"That chapter speaks about the Lord's return, right?"

"Yes."

Pastor Liviu's gaze was keen. "Do you have your notes with you?"

"I have them here in my Bible." Nicu opened his Bible and took out two sheets of paper. He watched Liviu's face closely as he read over the notes. At length Liviu looked up. "Would you be willing to preach tonight for ten minutes?"

Nicu didn't hesitate. "I'm willing." It was common for young men who'd been baptized to preach before the church. He followed the pastor to the front, where they sat down on the bench. During the singing, he studied his notes and prayed that God would speak to the people through his message.

At last Nicu walked up behind the pulpit. Opening his Bible and notes, he looked out over the crowd. For a moment the sea of eight hundred faces swam before him; and then, far away at the back of the room, one face came sharply into focus.

What is he doing here? Caught off guard, Nicu swallowed. He saw the second director of the boarding school every day—but never before at church! *Either he's a Christian, or he's here to see who's attending.*

Gripping the edge of the pulpit, Nicu spoke, his voice strong and steady. "I greet you in Jesus' name. I would like to read in Matthew 24."

Director Marion walked down the street, the passage Nicu had read still ringing in his ears. "Watch therefore: for ye know not what hour your Lord doth come. . . . Therefore be ye also ready: for in such an hour as ye think not the Son of man cometh. . . . But and if that evil servant shall say in his heart, My lord delayeth his coming . . . the lord of that servant shall come in a day when he looketh not for him, and in an hour that he is not aware of, and shall cut him asunder, and appoint him his portion with the hypocrites: there shall be weeping and gnashing of teeth."

It was clear that Nicu believed the words he had preached. How many seventeen-year-old boys had such a strong faith? Deep in thought, the director opened his home gate. He slept little that night. By morning he had made up his mind. He would send for Nicu and talk to him personally in his office on Monday.

The footsteps that came up the stairs on Monday were quick and unfaltering, and Nicu's dark eyes were fearless as he walked into the room. Behind the desk, Marion cleared his throat. "How did you get to church?" he asked.

Nicu's clear gaze met his. "I went through a window."

The director cleared his throat once more. "If you want to go to church again, come to me and I'll give you a permission slip."

"Thank you, sir."

"You are dismissed."

Nicu closed the door quietly, wondering what was going through the director's mind. Marion carried himself with dignity and took life seriously. Had he grown up in a Christian family? Did he know Christ as his Lord and Savior?

Nicu never saw Marion at church again. As the days went by, he prayed often for his school director.

Nicu was eighteen, with a steady, straight-forward gaze, the boyish lines in his face maturing into young manhood. As he stood on the platform to receive his graduation diploma, Nicu felt a mixture of sadness and anticipation in his heart. The past four years had done much to broaden his horizons and mold his character. A chapter in his life was closing, but a new one was opening. What lay in the years ahead? What sorrows would he have to face? What joys?

Several months later Nicu visited Pastor Liviu at his house. "As long as you keep your eyes on Jesus, you'll be able to stand strong through whatever comes your way," the pastor told him. "It's the key to success in life."

"That's what I want to do," Nicu responded. "But I find that I have to be constantly on guard."

"The enemy is real," Liviu agreed thoughtfully. "He's out to get us in any way he can, but God is able to keep us." Leaning back in his chair, he changed the subject. "Tell me what has been happening in your life, Nicu."

Nicu took a sip of the coffee that Liviu's wife had served them. "After I graduated, I started working full-time in the factory. It's huge! Around 7,000 workers, all building cranes and machines. My job is to put certain parts together."

"I'm sure you don't go home as often as your parents would like."

Nicu smiled a little. "That's true. I wish I could be with my family more often."

They sat in companionable silence for a few minutes. Nicu always enjoyed his visits with Liviu Olah. The pastor had good insights and encouraged him in his Christian life.

"I have a question for you, Nicu." Liviu's voice broke into his thoughts. "Would you be willing to be a leader for church youth? You'd be in charge of going out into the villages and doing missionary work, among other things."

Nicu couldn't speak for a moment. Liviu was asking him to be a leader over two hundred young people! What did the pastor see in him that made him think he was capable?

"I believe you can do it," Liviu was saying. "Your faith in God is strong, and it shines in everything you do. You have the ability to lead."

Silence fell between them for a long moment. At length Nicu lifted his head. "If you think I can do it, I'm willing."

Liviu smiled and placed a hand on his shoulder. "Let's pray together right now, Nicu." He closed his eyes. "Dear Lord, I pray that you will bless this young man and give him strength as he takes over these responsibilities. May he always look to you for guidance and be a blessing to those around him. In Jesus' name. Amen."

The words flowed over Nicu like a benediction. When he finally stood to leave, the pastor clasped his hand warmly. "God be with you, son."

"And with you, pastor." Nicu returned the warm clasp, still feeling humbled. This pastor who had baptized him and mentored him was leaving a great impact on his life.

6

"Trust in the Lord"

Two hundred young voices rang out in the stillness of the winter air. Snow adorned roofs up and down the street, and lighted apartment windows revealed faces listening to the young people. The night was clear, with stars shining and a radiant full moon.

Zipping her coat higher, Ana Monica Bejenaru glanced across the crowd of youth. From where she stood, she had a good view of everyone. At seventeen, she enjoyed the church youth activities. This night they had gone out into the streets after the church service to sing Christmas carols. Their voices could be heard everywhere in the snowy night.

When they were finished singing, the audience began clapping from the open windows. "Let us give you something to drink," a man called from the closest window. "We're having a party in here, and there's plenty of alcohol for everyone."

"We don't drink, sir," Monica heard her brother Octavian call out.

"But we do invite you to come to our church tomorrow," Nicu Craiovan added, stepping forward. "We're planning to have a Christmas program." Turning to the other lighted windows along the street, he raised his voice. "This invitation stands for everyone! Come to church tomorrow and celebrate the birth of Christ with us!"

As the youth moved on, Monica wondered how people would respond to Nicu's invitation. She had noticed how active he was in the work of the Lord, and she felt he was a person of integrity. He spoke with authority and had an upright character. But would the people really come to the church service the next day?

Morning revealed the answer. From her place in the choir, Monica recognized many people from the night before crowding the church pews. As the director led them in singing "Joy to the World," the faces in the audience grew softer, as if their hearts were indeed receiving the heavenly King.

"How did Nicu do it?" Rodica asked after the service was over. "He invited the people, and they all came!" Monica was talking with three of her close friends who sang in the choir with her.

"He's well-known in the villages for doing missionary work," Estera said.

"Yes, that's right," Lidia confirmed. "He preaches the Gospel and prays with a lot of people."

Monica was silent as her friends talked on. She knew that many girls considered Nicu one of the finest young men in the youth group. Nice-looking and friendly, he knew the Bible well and was active in the church, preaching, reciting poems, and boldly praying when church members prayed audibly during services. He was in charge of activities for more than two hundred youth, and he was zealous in going out into surrounding villages and doing missionary work. She didn't know many like him.

Glancing at her watch, she announced, "I have to go. See you girls later." Clutching her song folder, she moved down the aisle. Groups of people filled the entry, and through the open doors she could see snowflakes drifting down, glinting in the sunlight.

"May I walk you home?"

Monica glanced up, startled. This wasn't the first time she had been asked that question, but never by Ştefan. She hesitated. It was common knowledge that when a boy asked to walk a girl home, he had something serious in mind. And as far as she knew, this good-looking young man was a sincere Christian. It was only polite to accept at least once. "Okay," she said with a smile. "Let me get my coat, and then I'll be ready."

Minutes later they moved through the door together and down the street. "That was quite a service today, wasn't it?" Ștefan remarked.

"I was amazed by how many people actually showed up." Monica shivered as the wind picked up. Tying her scarf tighter, she added, "It's sad that they'll be going right back to the life they've been living before."

Ștefan looked serious. "Maybe the service today touched someone's heart."

They walked on, their conversation drifting from one thing to another. It was easy to talk to Ștefan, but by the time he left her at the door, Monica knew she would not be accepting any more proposals from him. Ștefan was nice and had a good testimony, but she didn't feel he was the one she wanted in her life.

In her room that night, Monica spent extra time in prayer during her personal devotions. "More than anything, Lord, I want your will to be done in my life," she whispered. "Please help me to keep my heart for you alone. If there is someone for me, I trust you to lead us together in your perfect timing."

Peace stole into her heart, assuring her that God was indeed in control of her life. With a smile she closed her Bible and climbed into bed.

Nicu sat at his desk, gazing unseeingly at the open Bible before him. Today was his birthday. Where had the time gone? He was twenty-one now, and it didn't seem long since his childhood. It was hard to believe that some men were married by this age.

Lifting his head, Nicu stared out the window. He wasn't blind to how several of the youth girls felt about him, but only one stood out. With her brown hair, hazel eyes, and sweet smile, Ana Monica Bejenaru was beautiful. She sang in the choir and had a peaceful soul. He admired the latter quality most of all. When he chose a wife, he wanted to look at the heart, and not only the beauty.

But would Monica accept him?

Nicu shifted restlessly. Other young men had tried to begin a relationship with Monica, and it hadn't worked out. Who was he to think it would be any different for him? But he had been thinking about this for a while already, making it a matter of prayer. What did God want him to do?

His glance fell on the Bible again. "Trust in the LORD with all thine heart; and lean not unto thine own understanding. In all thy ways acknowledge him, and he shall direct thy paths."

Bowing his head, Nicu began to pray. He remained in that position for a long time.

Monica felt as though her heart was singing a summer song with the birds as she slipped out of her home gate. The choir always met early to practice before church, and this Sunday evening was perfect for a stroll.

Besides, she wanted to spend some time alone with God. Was He leading her to marry Nicolae Craiovan? They had been walking home from church together for a month now, and as she had learned to know him better, she discovered that this young man had high ideals. Out of all the girls, why had he chosen her? Could she ever measure up to what he was looking for in a wife?

Nicu was burning for the work of the Lord; she knew that. And their courtship was clean and pure. "I can see your hand in this, Lord," she whispered, looking up toward the sky. "But more than anything, I want your will to be done. Is this from you? Help me to trust your leading!"

Twilight was stealing across the land when Nicu and Monica left the church together after the service. "I was blessed by the baptismal service today," Nicu said. "Pastor Liviu always preaches such stirring messages."

Monica smiled. "I felt great joy when I was baptized." Crickets were starting to sing, and early stars were appearing. It felt right to be walking with Nicu, discussing the day's events.

"It's been several years since I was baptized, but it was a happy day for me too," Nicu was saying.

"Pastor Liviu baptized you, didn't he?"

"Yes. He has influenced me greatly. So many people have impacted my life—some just through stories I've heard. I never knew my grandfather, but I know he was a warrior for God."

"Did you hear stories about him as a child?"

Nicu nodded. "When my *bunicu* (grandfather) was young, he served in the army. There was a minister who talked to them, and Bunicu became a believer. When he went home, he started preaching on the streets and in houses. He walked up and down hills to visit churches in all kinds of weather!"

Monica smiled. It sounded like the young man walking beside her. "How did he die?" she asked softly.

"He died in 1947 while preaching behind the pulpit. That was here in Timișoara, where the yearly church meeting was being held in a Baptist church. It was a shock to everyone," Nicu added quietly. "The last words of Bunicu's message were, 'And be not conformed to this world: but be ye transformed by the renewing of your mind, that ye may prove what is that good, and acceptable, and perfect, will of God.' When his daughter Ana saw him die, she received such a shock that she never recovered. She died five months later; she was only sixteen years old."

"So young," Monica murmured. "How sad!"

"My grandfather was only fifty-two years old when he died, but his life had been busy and fulfilling," Nicu explained. "When one of the churches was closed, it was a great blow to him. It even affected his health." He paused and grinned at her. "I've always thought I have a good heritage."

She smiled back. "It is inspiring. My grandfather on Mama's side was also a church leader. He preached and directed the chorus. During World War I, Hungarian soldiers came and set their house on fire, forcing them to leave. My mother's family fled here to Timișoara, and this is where I grew up."

"What was your childhood like?" Nicu wondered.

Monica's eyes took on a reflective look. "I had a good childhood, and I grew up with singing and prayer. Mama taught us not to speak negatively about anyone. If we didn't have a good thing to say, we were to stay quiet!

"My grandfather on my *tata's* side also gave me a good heritage," she went on reflectively. "My parents told me the story of when the government took my *bunicu's* land away. Bunicu's family moved to the collective farm, but there was hardly enough food to survive.

"The government had taken their corn and potatoes, but Bunicu still had a bag of wheat. He wanted to keep his wheat safe, so he prayed, 'Lord, if I hide this big bag of wheat, they'll find it. But if *you* hide it, they won't find it.'

"Then the thought came to Bunicu to put this bag of wheat under a nut tree in the vegetable garden. That night snow covered everything, hiding all the tracks he had made. When the soldiers came, they searched everywhere except under that tree. They couldn't find anything, and finally they left."

Nicu smiled. "What a story! It strengthens my faith."

Monica nodded. "Bunicu taught his faith to Tata. When Tata broke his back in a work-related accident and became unable to work, he felt he wasn't worth much anymore. But he became full of spiritual strength. I was young when he told us we need to give all our fears to the Lord, because He can take care of them. 'God makes no mistakes,' he told me. That made a great impression on me."

They had reached Monica's home gate by now. Darkness was deepening all around them as more creatures joined the night's chorus. "I'll say good night here," Nicu said, smiling. Because of his convictions, he never came into the house alone with her, and Monica respected him for it. "May I see you next week?"

Glancing up, she smiled shyly. "You may. Good night."

"Good night, Monica." Nicu closed the gate and turned to walk homeward, joy filling his heart. Monica's gentle, virtuous character inspired him to be the best he could be for her sake. The Bible verses he had read before he started asking to walk her home came to his mind again. "Trust in the LORD with all thine heart, and lean not unto thine own understanding. In all thy ways acknowledge him . . . "

Glancing toward the starry heavens, Nicu offered a silent prayer. *I want to keep trusting you for direction in my future, dear Lord. May your will be done.*

7

"Not My Will"

September of 1972 was painting the forests with gold, orange, and russet colors. The rustling fields waited for harvest, and flocks of geese flew south for winter. The plaintive note in their calls struck a responding chord in Nicu's heart one evening as he walked along the fields toward the village. Had a month ever passed by so slowly?

When he had asked Monica to marry him after several months of courtship, she had been hesitant. "Let me have one month," she had said. "I have to pray and ask God if it's His will for us to be together for life." Knowing that he would be forced to leave for military service in October, Nicu was eager to hear her answer. But he could do nothing except wait.

The flock of geese was flying into the sunset now, their bodies dark silhouettes against the glowing clouds. Nicu looked wistfully after them. Would the end of the month bring the answer his heart desired? "Not my will but thine be done, Lord," he whispered.

Landscape rushed by in a blur outside the train window. Leaning her head against the back of the seat, Monica closed her eyes in silent prayer. *Am I doing the right thing in asking for these signs, Lord? I long to have your assurance that Nicu is the one for me. I know he's dedicated to you, but this is such a big decision. I don't want to make a mistake!*

By now Monica knew she would have her parents' blessing if she decided to marry Nicu. But she was still unsure. The idea to ask for a sign had come one night the week before while she had been reading her Bible and praying. Glancing up, her gaze had fallen on a book that Nicu had loaned her. She had agreed that she would return it in two weeks. Reaching for the book, she had turned it over in her hand. *Dear Lord, tomorrow is Sunday, and Nicu and I will be walking home together from church. I'll give Nicu this book then, and if he tells me to keep it for myself, I'll take it as a sign that he is the one for me. It's something simple, but I need to know what your will is!*

Monica smiled. The young man who sought her heart had passed the first test—his book had gone home with her again and was now at home on her desk. But she still wasn't satisfied. As the train sped on, taking her to the city where she planned to spend the day, Monica reviewed the second sign she had decided to look for. "My uncle is very sick," Nicu had told her the Sunday before. "We think he's in the last days of his cancer. I'm planning to start staying with him, so we can't see each other this week."

It was Thursday now, and they had not seen each other. It was getting rather late in the week, but she hadn't given up hope yet. *If Nicu comes to see me anyway this week, I'll take it as another sign that he's the one for me.*

The train slowed, breaking into her reverie. Monica stood up, shouldering her purse. Descending the steps, she left the train station and headed out into the streets. Appetizing aromas wafted from various restaurants, reminding her that it was time to eat. But today she had decided it was more important to fast and pray for the Lord's will.

After doing her business in the city, Monica took the train home again. By the time she had walked to her gate, night had fallen. Monica found her parents in the kitchen, sipping cups of tea. "Monica! You look exhausted," exclaimed her mother, standing up. "Sit down and let me warm up something for you to eat."

"Thanks, Mama." Sinking into a chair, Monica rubbed her temples. "I am really tired and hungry. I was fasting most of the day."

Jacob Bejenaru looked at his daughter with concern. "I know you wanted to wait a month to answer Nicu's request, but I'm afraid it's hard on you."

Monica smiled. "Don't worry about me. I can feel that my faith is being strengthened through this."

"Here you are." Ana set a dish of cornmeal on the table before her daughter. "I'll get you some tea too."

Monica watched her mother fondly as she bustled toward the stove. The cornmeal was warm and delicious, and the aroma of tea made the kitchen seem homey. It felt good to relax with her parents.

"Nicu stopped by today," Tata said, leaning back in his chair.

Monica glanced up sharply. "He did?"

Tata's eyes twinkled. "He was looking for you."

That was all Monica needed to hear. As she closed her bedroom door minutes later, her heart sang. Though she didn't want to base her decision to marry Nicu on these signs alone, they were so helpful, giving her assurance that everything was indeed coming from God. He made no mistakes, and it was safe to trust Him with her life.

The evening Monica gave Nicu her answer was filled with smiles. The long month of waiting was over, and the future stretched before them, bright with promise.

Several clouds appeared on the horizon, however. In October Nicu would be leaving to spend a year and four months in military service. All young Romanian men were forced to go—if they resisted, they could be imprisoned. But tonight it didn't matter. They were together, and that was enough.

Before they parted, Nicu had one last request for this beautiful young lady who had finally promised to be his wife. "The next time we meet, you bring a list of what you expect from me after we get married, and I'll bring a list of what I expect from you. Is that all right?"

"It sounds rather scary," she admitted. "What if I disappoint you?"

He laughed a little. "We will probably both disappoint each other. Marriage is for life, and we'll get to know every aspect of each other." His eyes shone as he added, "But with God's help, I'm willing to make that commitment."

"So am I," she answered softly.

Nicu sat at his desk, pen in hand. The paper before him lay empty, but he knew how he wanted to fill it. He turned the pages of his Bible thoughtfully. He couldn't imagine Monica falling short in any of the attributes of love listed in 1 Corinthians 13. But as he had told her, marriage was for life, and they would get to know each other inside out. Could they always adhere to this chapter? *Love is longsuffering, always kind, doesn't envy, isn't easily angered . . .*

Nicu's gaze lingered on the passage as he thought about everything it meant. They would be joined in marriage and become one for life. To build their marriage on this chapter and stay with it until death required a firm, unshakeable commitment to each other and to God. But with Christ as the head of their home, they would have a threefold cord that could not be quickly broken.

With a steady hand, Nicu fell to writing. He lost track of time until a knock sounded on the door, and it opened almost at once. "Nicu? Are you here?"

"Mama!" Crossing the room quickly, he folded her in his arms. "And Tata!" He embraced his father next. "It's so good to see you!" His brothers crowded in behind them, turning the quiet room into a joyful, noisy place.

"I'm eager to see this girl you keep talking about," Samuel said teasingly, slapping him on the back.

Nicu laughed. "And I'm eager for you to meet her." Because of traveling difficulties, his family had never met Monica before. They were planning to announce their engagement formally that night to both families.

Half an hour later they all sat down to a delicious meal that Monica and her mother had prepared. In accordance with Nicu's high standards, Monica's mother sat between the engaged couple at the table. The pastor was also there to give the blessings. The evening flew by, and Nicu did not find himself alone with Monica until he was ready to leave again.

"Well, where's your list?" he asked, smiling, as they stood together by the door. He felt reluctant to leave this celebration, held hundreds of times for other people, but never before for the two of them. What would Monica require of him? She was worthy of everything good and pure and beautiful. Could he truly give her what she needed?

Monica's trusting gaze met his. "I don't have a list. There's only one thing I ask—that you remain how you are."

For a moment he could not reply. "You honor me, Monica," he said at length, his voice a little husky. "But I want to strive to be better—to be the best I can, for your sake." Reaching into his pocket, he unfolded his paper. "Here is what I wrote."

Monica caught her breath as her glance fell on the page. Nicu had written a long list. As she read the words from 1 Corinthians 13, color crept into her cheeks. "This looks scary," she confessed, looking up. "There's a lot to live up to. But I'll do my best to always be what it says."

"That's all I ask," he said softly. "I'm making this promise right along with you."

As dusk deepened outside and stars studded the heavens, Nicu and Monica came before God in prayer, asking Him to bless and guide them as they pledged their lives to each other. By His grace alone would they be able to enter this new realm of life and travel its pathway.

8

"In the Army, All Are Soldiers"

Laughter filled the train car, mingling with the odors of smoke and alcohol being passed around freely. Nicu stared out the window, taking no notice of the activity around him. They had been traveling all day from Timișoara to the city of Iași, where he would be serving compulsory time in military training. It had been so hard to say goodbye to his family and friends, knowing it would likely be a long time before he would see them again. Eight hundred kilometers equaled a fourteen-hour trip, and the sixteen months he would be away seemed to stretch into infinity.

It had been hardest of all to say goodbye to the sweet girl he loved. They were planning to write, but the year ahead could not pass by quickly enough. *Oh, God, please be with me,* he breathed silently. *Help me to be strong and—*

An outburst of laughter from behind him broke into his prayer. Nicu sighed a little and sank deeper into his seat. The train was filled with fifty young men, all set to have a good time. This particular group surrounded the army captain, laughing and exchanging jokes. Nicu turned his gaze toward the window. Twilight was stealing across the land, and he knew they would be traveling through the night.

Nicu leaned closer to the window, watching the landscape rush past in a blur. What would he face this year? He knew his parents would pray for him, and Monica had also promised to keep him in her prayers. He was going to need those prayers; he wasn't in the best of health. But no matter what the future held, he was confident that the Lord would see him through. Did He not promise in His Word to never leave or forsake him? "Fear thou not; for I am with thee," God had said in Isaiah. "Be not dismayed; for I am thy God: I will strengthen thee; yea, I will help thee; yea, I will uphold thee with the right hand of my righteousness."

Nicu closed his eyes, praying silently as peace stole into his heart. God's presence engulfed him, and he relaxed.

After one day and night on the train, the boys reached Iaşi. There they were taken to the army camp and forced to dress like soldiers, with uniforms and shaved hair. As they stood at attention, giving their names one by one to the army officer for registration, Nicu was startled to hear a familiar voice across the room. He hadn't seen Costică on the train, but he knew the man's parents from church. Costică did not attend services regularly.

When the boys were dismissed, Nicu made his way toward Costică through the crowd. "It's good to see a familiar face here," he said with a grin. "Where were you sitting on the train?"

"I was in the group with the captain." Costică looked different, dressed in his army uniform and cap.

"Really? I didn't notice you."

"We were trying to be friends with the captain," Costică said, shrugging. "He has a high position in the army, you know."

"So did you become friends?"

Costică seemed to hesitate. "He was easy to get along with. We gave him some alcohol and he got drunk." He stopped short, looking a little ashamed. "I'd like to work in the colonel's office," he said, changing the subject abruptly.

Nicu knew what he meant. The group of fifty men had been tested for

"IN THE ARMY, ALL ARE SOLDIERS"

the best penmanship when they had arrived. Whoever was chosen would work for the colonel, who was under the highest commander in the army and needed a secretary.

"I'm sure we'll hear who's chosen soon enough," Nicu remarked. It was clear that Costică did not stand for Christ, although he came from a Repentant family.

"As you know, the colonel needs a secretary." The army major met the captain's gaze. "We have tested the fifty men brought from Timişoara to see who has the best penmanship for the job. Of them all, Nicu Craiovan has the best handwriting." He paused, glancing at the file in his hand. "But he is a Repentant."

The captain weighed his words before speaking. "Nicu has the best handwriting, but I have another man who can work for the colonel."

"Who are you suggesting?"

"His name is Costică."

The major paged through the files, then stopped. He studied the page silently for a moment. "Costică's file says nothing about his religion. Is he not a Repentant?"

"No." The captain didn't mention how Costică and the boys had befriended him during the long train ride from Timişoara to Iaşi. Nor did he mention the alcohol they had given him or the jokes they had exchanged. But there was no doubt in his mind—the boy was not a Christian.

The major sat thinking. "Very well," he said at length. "We will ask Costică to work for the colonel instead of Nicu."

"You won't regret it, officer. Costică will do a fine job."

The major looked up. "Did Nicu cause problems on the way here?"

"No," he answered quickly. "Not at all. But I think there's a better place for him."

"That may well be," said the major, nodding. "Good day."

Opening the office door, the captain saluted. "Good day, sir."

The room was filled with soldiers all standing in place, eyes riveted on their instructor, Nicu Craiovan. The major stood at the back of the room, watching and taking notes. The boys who came to the military spent the first three months in school, where they received training to be leaders. Nicu had been brought to the base several weeks ago, where he had begun instructing new soldiers in what he had learned. It was instruction time now, and the major had come to see how Nicu was doing.

The next morning he sent for Nicu. "I want to talk with you about what I observed yesterday."

"Yes, sir." Nicu sounded calm, but there was a question in his eyes.

The major went straight to the point. "You have a gift for leadership, Craiovan. It is clear that you are obedient to authority."

Nicu smiled a little. "I grew up under my father this way, sir. When he told us to do something, we were expected to do it instantly, and do it right."

The major leaned forward. "We need a person like you, Craiovan, to be active and obey what you're asked to do. I've decided to send you to a school where you'll be trained for a higher position in the army. You have a gift for commanding and giving orders, and I want to see you become even better in this work."

Something shifted in Nicu's clear dark eyes, and the major knew what his answer would be even before he spoke. "I'd rather not do that, sir."

"In the army, all are soldiers." The major's voice was firm, reminding him that soldiers were to obey their authorities without question.

Nicu hesitated and then straightened his shoulders. "Please don't send me there, sir," he said respectfully. "I have some health problems, and I'm

"IN THE ARMY, ALL ARE SOLDIERS"

not sure that it would be good for me. Won't you send me to the medical school instead?"

The major shook his head. "It's not possible. You will do as I have told you." He paused, and his tone softened slightly. "In January you'll receive further details about this. You are dismissed."

"Yes, sir." The young man opened the door quietly and stepped out of the office. Still leaning forward across his desk, the major watched him go. He shook his head. It was absurd that Nicolae Craiovan wanted to throw this opportunity away. He had the potential to become one of the best commanders in the army.

Nicu walked slowly down the hall, his thoughts whirling. It was true that he wasn't in the best of health, but he had been thinking of much more than that when he had declined the position the major wanted him to take. It was grueling work; besides, he wanted no part in the fighting if war actually did come. He shuddered at the very thought of killing a person. It went directly against God's commandments. He would much rather learn how to help those who were wounded on the battlefield.

Yet what could he do? In the army soldiers didn't have the right to ask for what they wanted. If only he could have helped the colonel instead of Costică. He would even welcome a job as a cook. But he could not choose. If he didn't find a way to go to medical school, he would have to obey the major's orders.

What did God want him to do? Unless He intervened with the major's plans, there was no way out of this. Nicu slipped into his dorm, glancing out the window. It was dark now, but he wouldn't be on duty to keep watch until midnight.

He lay awake for a long time, staring into the darkness. Was there absolutely nothing he could do? Going to an officer closer to his own rank had

63

availed nothing. "I won't do it," the officer had declared when Nicu asked him to go to the major and put in a good word for him. They were determined to increase his rank in the army.

Outside, the wind picked up, swirling snow against the window. It would soon be Christmas, and Nicu had heard many of the soldiers talking about home. How he would love to go home for Christmas! They had always tried to be together as a family for that special day, but he wasn't going to make it this year. In his mind's eye he could picture Mama, her face flushed and happy as she prepared the traditional dinner. Tata, tall at the head of the table as he led in prayer. His brothers, reciting poems and singing by the door.

He thought of Monica—of the sweet, unpretentious beauty that came from within and crowned her womanhood. How wonderful it would be to see her again! Letters simply weren't the same as seeing each other face to face, though they wrote almost daily. As he watched the swirling snow through the window, Nicu's thoughts turned heavenward once again. *Oh, God, I need your help. I don't want to go to this school for training to be a commander in the army. Please show me what I can do to move the major's heart!*

As soon as the clock struck midnight, Nicu slid out of bed. In the bunks around him, he could hear the soft breathing and snores of other soldiers as they slept. Carefully lifting his mattress, he felt underneath. Yes—there it was—his fingers were touching something small and hard. In a moment the New Testament was in his hand, glinting in the moonlight that slanted through the window.

The soldiers weren't allowed to have Christian books, and Nicu kept his Bible under the mattress. Only when no one was around could he read it, mostly when he was on watch from midnight to 3:00 a.m. Slipping the book into his pocket, Nicu went out the door to exchange places with the other guard on duty.

It was while he was reading the Gospel of Luke that an idea began to take shape in Nicu's mind. Perhaps he could write home and ask for something to take to the major as a Christmas gift. It was the only thing he could think of to try. *If this doesn't work—*

Nicu shut off the rest of the thought and read the verse in Luke 18:27 again. "The things which are impossible with men are possible with God." He would have to commit this into God's hands and trust Him for the outcome.

9

The Answer

Snowflakes fell fast and thick to the ground, nearly blinding Nicu as he turned his face into the wind. He glanced at the package in his hand. At his request, his mother had sent him two sets of six knives he had made earlier in the factory. He was taking them now to the major as a Christmas gift.

Sudden apprehension gripped him, and Nicu closed his eyes tightly. How would this turn out? Unless God moved the major's heart, it wasn't going to work.

The stairway that led up to the major's office was empty. Outside the door, Nicu hesitated, bowing his head in a brief prayer. Then he reached out and knocked.

"Craiovan?" The major met him at the door. "You wished to see me?"

"I did, sir." Nicu stepped inside, smiling. "I wanted to wish you a happy Christmas and bring you a little gift."

"Thank you." The words were sincere, but Nicu caught the major's quick glance. Taking the gift, he walked around behind his desk and sat down in the chair. He placed the package on the desk and gazed at it for a moment in meaningful silence. At last he looked straight into Nicu's eyes and spoke again, his voice quiet. "What do you want from me?"

Nicu didn't hesitate with his answer. "I want to go to medical school."

The major's brow furrowed, and he looked away. "I cannot promise," he said at length. "Go, and I'll think about it." Without doubt, he had seen right through the Christmas gift. What would he decide? There was nothing Nicu could do but wait.

"You'll go to medical school, Craiovan."

As the officer paused, Nicu's spirits soared. Could this be the same man who had refused to approach the major and put in a good word for him? Now his gruff tone was almost genial.

"You realize that permission for this has not been granted easily," the officer went on, looking at him closely.

"Yes, sir." How could this officer know what had really moved the heart of the major? As he left the office minutes later, Nicu's heart filled with a song of thanksgiving. Once again, God had worked on his behalf, making a way for him to avoid harming his fellowmen.[6]

The room was overflowing with soldiers, officers, and their wives. Nicu felt his throat tighten as he stood on the platform, gazing out across the crowd. Could he recite this poem without breaking down?

It was March now—three months since he had first started attending medical school. He had thrown himself into his studies and would soon be sent to an army camp in Bucharest for another three months. Today, however, this was the furthest thing from his mind. March 8 was Women's Day. What was his own mother doing right now? If only he could be at home with her! But he would honor her with the church poem he planned to recite.

---

[6] As a conservative Anabaptist publisher that believes the Scriptural teaching on nonresistance, we do not support military participation in any form. However, we can appreciate Nicu's exemplary behavior while in service: his effort to avoid becoming a commander, opting rather to study in the medical field; his diligent study of the Word; and his aversion to the thought of killing people.

Stepping forward, he began to speak in a clear, strong voice. All eyes focused on him, and as he recited, Nicu noticed tears beginning to mist the eyes of the officers' wives. What were their lives like? In this communist country, were any of them raising their children in the nurture and admonition of the Lord?

What kind of mothers did his fellow soldiers have? Did they pray for their sons? He couldn't be thankful enough for a mother who had taught him about God from earliest childhood. Her influence had laid the foundation for his choice to serve God at a tender age.

There were other godly ladies who had influenced him as well. How clearly he remembered the two single ladies from church who had prayed that he would preach the Gospel someday! He had been only eight years old then, but their prayer had made a deep impression on him.

Another certain young lady was also largely responsible for putting his heart in the right place. As the months passed by, Monica's letters were revealing more and more of her heart to him, and he was discovering within her peaceful soul the attributes of love, grace, and total dedication to God. For the sake of these virtuous women who had impacted his life, he wanted to reach the highest standard of godly manhood.

Nicu reached the concluding line of the poem. A hush fell over the room, and all the ladies were crying. Tears stinging his own eyes, Nicu finished reciting and stepped down from the platform.

"I was so happy for you when I found out that you were allowed to go to medical school." Monica's eyes shone as she brushed a stray strand of hair from her face. Sunlight slanted through the window, bringing out green flecks in her hazel eyes.

Nicu smiled. "I can't tell you how happy I was myself."

"And you were there for three months, right?" She leaned back in her chair.

"Yes. After that I was sent to another camp in Bucharest, and now I'm back here in Iași to finish my term." He grinned at her. "But your visit is the best part of these sixteen months."

She laughed. "You haven't served your full time yet. And it isn't just me who came to visit. If my mother hadn't come along, I wouldn't be here at all."

"I know." Nicu glanced toward Monica's mother, who was sitting across the room. "I'm very thankful she came with you." His voice quieted. "I wish I could see folks from home more often."

She looked at him with sympathy. "I'm sure you miss your family."

He nodded. "We're allowed to go home only once for fifteen days while we're here. But there's plenty to keep me busy, so that helps keep my mind occupied."

"It's July now," she mused. "You've been here nine months."

"And it's another seven months before I come home." He searched her face. "Has it felt long for you?"

She nodded, her cheeks coloring slightly. "Yes, it has. But I keep busy with my seamstress job at the factory, so that makes it bearable. And your letters help a lot. How has the waiting been for you?"

"Well, let's just say I was the happiest person in Iași when you told me you were coming." The gleam in his eyes made Monica smile. "But like I said, they keep us well-occupied here," he added. "I guess I should be thankful for that. When I think of our future together, it seems like a long, long time away."

"God has work for us to do between now and then," she said softly.

"I know. But I can't wait for the time to come when we'll be able to serve Him together," he answered, beaming.

10

A New Era

"Let me get this straight, Monica. Nicu came back from his term of service in February, and you're already getting married in April?"

Monica smiled at the incredulity in her sister's voice. "We first set the date in July and then changed it to June. Now we have our wedding day planned for April 28. It was too long to wait!"

Emanuela shook her head. "You don't have much time to plan."

"I know. The civil wedding is on April first, when we'll plan everything with the officials. We have to do medical tests and paperwork—but I guess you know all that already." The papers they would sign at the civil wedding would proclaim them married, but Monica knew that her relationship with Nicu would remain unchanged. Only after the church wedding would they consider themselves officially married.

Settling deeper into the train seat, she glanced out the window. "I'm so glad it worked for you to go shopping with me today," she said, turning back to Emanuela. "When you got married last year, I saw firsthand how much work goes into a wedding. I'm pretty nervous about it all."

"There is a lot to prepare," her sister agreed. "I hope Nicu is ready for that."

Monica sobered. Because her father wasn't well, much of the preparation would indeed fall on Nicu's shoulders. "I think he is. But I'll do what

I can to help him. Both of us have been saving money for this, and Nicu's father will provide some money and food. As for me, I have lots of details to attend to. Besides shopping for new shoes today, there are other things I need to get. I'm glad for any help you can give me."

Emanuela glanced at her. "What are you planning to do about a dress?"

Monica hesitated. "I'm not sure. We don't have enough money to buy a wedding dress for me and a new suit for Nicu, plus pay for all the food."

"Then you might welcome my offer," Emanuela said quietly. "I've only worn my wedding dress and veil once, Monica. If you want to try it on, I'll bring it over tomorrow afternoon. We're the same size, so it should fit you perfectly. Consider it my gift for your wedding."

Relief shone in Monica's eyes. "Thank you, Emanuela," she said. "We'll gladly accept your offer." How like her older sister to do this! Emanuela's kind, giving heart had manifested itself in many ways throughout the years. Now she was doing all she could behind the scenes to make her younger sister's wedding day a success.

"Oh, God, come now with your blessing; oh, God, come now, and stay with us . . ."

The wedding song was a benediction and prayer all in one, swelling around the bride and groom as they walked slowly down the aisle to the front of the church. This day, April 28, 1974, was their special day, radiant with sunshine and consecrated with sacred beauty. Nicu and Monica were coming together to the marriage altar before God to pledge their lives to each other and become united for life.

Reaching the front of the church, they turned to face the crowd, standing until the choir finished singing. Nicu stole a glance at his bride, his heart swelling with emotion. Never had she looked lovelier. Slim and graceful in her long white dress, she wore a misty white veil and carried a bouquet of calla lilies. Could it be true that from this day on she would be his?

Catching his glance, Monica smiled into his eyes. From taking a morning photograph to preparing the room at the restaurant where they would have the reception, the hours up until then had been busy and tiring for her groom. But they were finally about to make their vows before God and these witnesses. They had kept themselves pure in heart and body, and this day marked the beginning of a new era in their lives.

After the choir finished singing, the couple took their seats in front of the congregation. A prayer and simple program followed. The singing groups, poem recitation, and wedding message passed in a blur. At last they stood together again before the pastor, his questions to them both ringing solemnly in the hushed sanctuary. Were they freely taking each other as man and wife? Would they be faithful to each other for better or for worse, in sickness and in health, forsaking all others until death parted them? Nicu's answers rang out firmly. Monica's voice was softer but still full of conviction, her eyes misting with tears. The Lord had truly come with His blessing, uniting them with the sacred vows that were being made before Him. In life's cloud or sun, His love would be their guide and stay.

The newlyweds did not go on a wedding trip. Unable to buy an apartment of their own for the time being, they moved in with Monica's parents. They made the third family in four rooms, with her parents, married sister, and brothers still living at home. Both Nicu and Monica kept their jobs and made applications at their factories to buy an apartment. Knowing it could be three to nine years before they received the right to buy, they waited and prayed and worked together.

Spring melted into summer, and summer into fall. Winter came with frigid winds and ice, but as he walked home through the snowy streets night after night, Nicu looked forward to the heartwarming smile that he knew would welcome him at the door. His evenings with Monica and her family were filled with light and love and laughter. Every day grew brighter, even when the winds blew and night fell early. When they found out that a baby would be added to their number in the spring, their joy increased even more.

The nippy March air chilled Nicu as he paced the street. He shivered, more from tension than the chill, and cast another anxious glance toward the hospital. This waiting was torture! Was Monica all right? When would he be able to see her and their new little one? He hadn't been able to go in with her for the delivery, but she had promised to hold up the baby by the window. Time had never seemed to stand so still as he waited.

But what was that now—a curtain fluttering at one of those second-story windows? Nicu stood still, his gaze riveted on it. That was Monica standing there—wasn't it? Yes, she was smiling down at him as she held up a small bundle to the window. The baby was wrapped in a blue blanket, and he could barely see the tiny face peeking out. Nicu glanced again at Monica, returning her smile with a broad grin and wave. God had given them a son!

Benjamin Sebastian, born on March 17, 1975, quickly became the apple of everyone's eye. When his father was around, however, no one else dared to hold Benjamin—Tata doted on his little son. Under his mother's care and surrounded by loving family, Benjamin grew strong and healthy, and life settled into a new normal.

"What do you think of it, Monica?" Nicu asked. "This apartment is small, but—"

"It might be small, but it's perfect!" Monica's eyes sparkled as she paused by the window to look outside. "We finally have our own home and more privacy. I'm excited about that."

Nicu joined her at the window, Benjamin in his arms. "Look out there, Benny. See all the people hurrying by?" Glancing at his wife, he added, "I'm excited about it too. Your parents have been really good to us, but I'm glad we can be on our own."

That summer, Monica had received approval from the factory where she worked to buy an apartment. Having both saved money from their jobs, Nicu and Monica had put it together and made their first payment on the apartment. It certainly had little space to spare, but it was theirs.

"I need to check on the food." Monica turned away from the window. "The table has to be set as well."

"Benny and I can set the table." Nicu ruffled a hand through Benjamin's brown hair, so much like his own. The four-month-old cooed and grinned up at him. "We're a good team, aren't we, son?"

Monica flashed a smile over her shoulder as she hurried away. Cabbage soup was simmering on the stove, and after she sliced a loaf of bread, they were ready to eat.

Nicu led in prayer, offering thanks to the God who had come with His blessing on their wedding day, and whose presence was staying with them as they traveled life's road together.

"The Lord has been good to us," Nicu remarked as they sat down. "We have our own home now, and we're surrounded by family and friends in the church."

Monica's eyes shadowed. "I can't help but wonder what is ahead for our church, Nicu."

He knew what she meant. The church had grown so much within the recent months that they had decided to start another church. The committee had asked Pastor Ioan Trif to open his house for church services, and there were 104 members, plus children, who attended. Ioan Trif was the pastor for both churches, and a new committee had been formed. At twenty-five, Nicu was the youngest of the nine members on the committee and had been delegated as the church secretary.

"You said it's almost impossible to get permission from the officials to start a new church?" Monica asked now.

"Yes, the inspector over the churches in the Timişoara district has already met with Pastor Ioan, trying to make him close his house to us. But the Lord made a way in that," Nicu continued. "Pastor Ioan said that he was only renting the property and couldn't make such a decision." He paused and then sighed a little. "But I know it isn't over yet."

Silence fell between them for a moment, broken by the sound of Benjamin banging his spoon against the table. At length Nicu spoke again, his voice soft. "God is not limited in what He can do. I truly believe He wants us to have this church."

Monica nodded, and the shadow in her eyes lightened. "I know. I just have to keep reminding myself that He is in control."

They dropped the topic then, but it lingered with Nicu that night as he spent time alone with God. What indeed was ahead for their church? It was illegal to form a separate group from the churches already accepted by the government. Among the committee members, Nicu was the most knowledgeable about the law. He had been working hard to receive permission from the officials. His greatest desire was to protect their church under the law in a Biblical way, but they couldn't have protection without authorization. And the way things were going, they would not be able to receive permission unless a miracle happened.

But he also believed his own words—that God was unlimited. Paging through his Bible, Nicu caught sight of a verse in Genesis 18: "Is any thing too hard for the LORD?" As he studied the words, his heart took new courage. If God wanted them to have this new church, He would see to it that the officials granted permission for it.

11

"We Will Not Close This Church"

"I should be home in a couple of hours, but if I'm not, don't wait up for me." Reaching for his Bible, Nicu turned to his wife. She stood by the door with Benjamin in her arms, watching him.

She met his gaze and then looked away. He stepped closer, studying her face. "Are you afraid, dear?"

She took a deep breath. "I'm uneasy, Nicu, and I can't help it. This meeting may not turn out well at all."

Nicu didn't answer. He knew quite well what could happen. "Let's pray together right now, shall we?" he suggested. Taking her hand, he bowed his head. "Dear Lord, please be with Monica and Benjamin tonight while I'm gone. Give Monica peace and strength. Be with us also as we meet with the inspector. May your will be done . . ."

"Amen," Monica said at the end of the prayer, and Nicu was relieved to see her smile. But he could still see the tension in her face as they said goodbye at the door. Walking out into the street, he paused at the corner to look back. She was standing by the window, watching him. He waited long enough to see her return his smile and wave, and then he turned the corner and hurried on.

He could understand Monica's fear. That night the church committee would meet with the inspector who supervised all the churches in the

Timișoara district. The inspector had been sent by the highest official of the Communist Party in Bucharest to force them to close their church. But Nicu was confident that God's power was greater than the power of the Communist Party members.

The inspector spoke forcefully, doing his utmost to compel the pastor and committee to close the church. Nicu sat quietly in his chair, listening as the discussion went on and on. Tension was mounting, and the inspector was growing agitated. Nicu could tell by the way he rapped out his words. "You can have religious freedom in the Baptist churches that are already accepted, but outside of this it's illegal to start a new church. You're trying to form a new party, and that is against the law!"

Nicu could keep silent no longer. Rising from his chair, he stepped forward. "We don't care about politics, sir," he said respectfully. "We are not making another party. We confess the Lord Jesus Christ. We present Him and want people to know Him." He opened his Bible. "In Acts 4:19-20 it says, 'But Peter and John answered and said unto them, Whether it be right in the sight of God to hearken unto you more than unto God, judge ye. For we cannot but speak the things which we have seen and heard.' "

He glanced up, looking straight into the inspector's eyes. "We must choose for ourselves what is right—to serve God or obey you. Is it better to obey you more than God? We can't quit talking about the things we have seen and heard."

Hot color flushed the inspector's cheeks, and Nicu knew he was thoroughly angry now. "There is no God! The things you have seen and heard"—his mouth twisted mockingly—"are myths!"

"They are not myths," Nicu answered steadily. "God has done wonderful things for His people. His power and might are recorded throughout the Scriptures, and we believe He is preparing a home for us in heaven."

"That's enough from you!" The inspector stood up, towering over Nicu. "If you don't calm down, I'll send you to prison!"

Nicu's clear gaze did not falter. "You can send me to prison; it doesn't matter. I am not doing politics. I am following the Bible and doing what it says."

The color in the inspector's cheeks heightened to a mottled purple. Twice he opened his mouth, but no words came out. Stepping quietly to Nicu's side, Pastor Ioan spoke in a calm, kind tone to the seething man. "Try to understand him, inspector. He's young and dynamic, and he is earnestly trying to be true to the Bible."

Taking a deep breath, the inspector sat down again. When he spoke, his voice was low and controlled, signaling that he was holding tight to his anger. "I'm telling you one last time. You must close this church, or there will be consequences."

But the committee's decision had already been made. They were not closing their church.

Soft lamplight spilled over the bedroom as Monica laid her sleeping baby in the crib. Stepping to the window, she looked out. It was 10:30 now, and Nicu still had not returned from the meeting. Her brow furrowed. Was something wrong? All evening she had been praying, unable to shake off her uneasiness.

Reaching for her Bible, Monica sat down on the bed. "Don't wait up for me," Nicu had said. Would her husband even come home? The question struck her with painful force, and her hands trembled as she turned to the Psalms.

> He that dwelleth in the secret place of the most High shall abide under the shadow of the Almighty. I will say of the LORD, He is my refuge and my fortress: my God; in him will I trust. . . . He shall cover thee with his feathers, and under his wings shalt thou trust: his truth shall be thy shield and buckler. Thou shalt not be afraid for the terror by night; nor for the arrow that flieth

by day. . . . Because thou hast made the LORD, which is my refuge, even the most High, thy habitation.

Monica studied the words until a measure of peace stole over her heart.

A full moon was shining as Nicu followed the pastor and other committee members through the door. He glanced toward the sky. Thousands of stars were twinkling like diamonds, but their beauty didn't seem to fit with what was happening. How long would they have to be at the police station for interrogation? Would he ever be able to go home again? Closing his eyes, he breathed a silent prayer. *This is in your hands, Lord. Give my dear wife peace in my absence, and help us to be faithful to you no matter what happens.*

The police station seemed as cold as the steely eyes of the officer who interrogated him in a separate room from the others. "Where have you come from? What are you doing? How did you get into this group?" The questions were fired at him, loud and demanding. Nicu chose his answers carefully, not flinching when the officer gave him a 5,000-lei fine. According to his salary, it would take up to two and a half months to pay the debt, but he was willing to do whatever it took for the sake of Christ and the church.

The next day Nicu stood before four hundred pairs of eyes belonging to his coworkers and factory supervisors. The supervisors had received orders from the police to question Nicolae Craiovan before all the workers, hoping to humiliate him and force him to close the new church. The interview had already been going on for several minutes, and there was an uncanny silence over the audience.

"He's a good worker, but he is on the Christian side and not the communist." The highest supervisor's voice rang out in the hushed room. Nicu knew that if this boss turned against him, he could be left without a job. The man was able to do as he pleased.

On the other side of Nicu, the lower employer seemed to hesitate. Then he straightened his shoulders and spoke in a quieter tone. "I don't have anything to say against him. He's a good person and a good worker." Nicu understood the tentativeness in the man's words. He could also lose his job by defending his employee.

The crowd was silent. Even if they appreciated Nicu, they could lose their jobs too if they spoke up in his defense. Everyone was afraid of the communist leaders, who had many ways to destroy a person's self-worth. They knew that the next day it could be them in this position. It wasn't safe to trust anyone. Even family members could report to the secret police if they had been persuaded to be informers. Each was afraid of his neighbor.

For a few minutes longer the boss questioned Nicu, trying to pressure him into obeying the government's command. But Nicu's answer was always the same—they were not going to close their church.

Nicu spent a long time on his knees that night in the cold room back at the police station. When was this all going to be over? What was his dear Monica going through? "Please have your will and way in this situation, Lord," he whispered. "Help us to know what to do and to look to you for courage. In Jesus' name I pray this . . ."

12

The Inspector's Decision

Monica stood at the window with her baby, watching the busy street below. Two days had passed since Nicu had left for the meeting. She had been notified about the reason for his detainment, and now the only thing she could think about was what could be happening to him at the police station. Was he all right? Would he have to go to prison? Would he ever come back? The haunting questions wrenched her heart.

Nicu had never been afraid to stand for what he believed. While she admired him for that, the uncertainty was wearing her down.

Tears filled her eyes as she planted a kiss on her son's soft cheek. *We must give our fears to God.* Never had her father's words from childhood held such meaning. How she wanted to give her fears to God—to trust and not be afraid. But it was harder than she had ever dreamed.

Slipping into the bedroom, she laid Benjamin on the bed and opened her Bible. She had often read through 1 Corinthians 13 since their marriage, striving to be the loving wife Nicu had asked her to be before their wedding day. " 'Beareth all things, believeth all things, hopeth all things, endureth all things,' " she whispered, her finger tracing verse seven. "Even this?" She buried her face in her hands, but she knew the beginning of the next verse by heart. *Charity never faileth.*

Glancing out the window, Monica gazed into the clear blue sky. "Oh,

God, please protect my husband today, wherever he is. Even if he never . . . comes home again—" Her voice broke completely, and tears fell down her cheeks. For a moment she could not go on. "Help me to be brave and support him in whatever he does for the church," she whispered at last. "May your will be done."

The church members gathered quietly and prayerfully for the meeting. Because of the committee's steadfast refusal to close their new church, an application had been made to the head government official from Bucharest for a permit. The inspector from Bucharest and local inspector from Timișoara were now meeting with all the members of the church to make the final decision. Nicu, sitting in front with the other committee members, felt at peace. They were ready for whatever opposition the inspectors might give. They had studied the constitution for the Baptist churches, and everything was prepared. The inspector from Bucharest had only to give his signature, and the work of the church could go on. After two days of relentless questions and ridicule, they would finally be allowed to return home.

But it quickly became apparent that the Bucharest inspector had no intention of giving his signature. "This church is illegal and has to be closed!" Telltale color spread across his cheekbones as he spoke.

Pastor Ioan Trif stood up. "Even if it's illegal, we will not close this church." Holding out both hands, he spoke earnestly. "Even if you put us in prison, we will not close it."

One of the other members stood to his feet. "Sir, it's illegal to put us in prison, because we have religious freedom in our church constitution." He gestured around the room, his voice respectful but firm. "We have a building, we are a group of Christians, and it's legal to have this church."

The inspector stiffened but seemed to realize he could not argue with these words. Coming down from the platform, he joined the other inspector, talking with him in low tones. The congregation waited silently, praying that God would move their hearts to give a favorable answer.

At last the inspector came forward again. "There are two conditions you must meet in order to receive a permit." His eyes were piercing as he looked over the committee members. "If you close this church for one month and remove Nicu Craiovan from the committee, you'll receive the permit for this organization."

Nicu stood up. "It's not a problem for me to leave the committee of the church," he said calmly. "But I won't sit down until you promise the permit." He paused, and the room grew completely still.

The inspector stared at the young man before him. Nicu stood erect, meeting his gaze without flinching. It was clear that the past two days of interrogation had not shaken his faith one bit. In fact, it seemed to have strengthened it—he was clearly willing to do whatever it took for the sake of his church. Where did such courage come from?

At last the inspector cleared his throat and spoke directly to Nicu. "We promise."

"I know they wanted me to come off the committee because I'm the secretary of the church," Nicu said to Monica that night. "But I wasn't going to sit down until they gave their promise. So often the government officials don't keep their promises."

Monica's expression was thoughtful. "I wonder what their reason is for making us close the church for a month."

"They have the power to do anything," he reminded her. "But we're going to take turns watching the building this month. We want to make sure they'll keep their word. And in the meantime," he added, smiling, "we'll attend the church we were a part of before this new one started."

"It'll be good to go back," Monica said with a smile.

At the end of the month, the head official over the Baptist churches granted the permit, and they began holding services regularly in the new church. Nicu was asked to remain on the committee, but only as a member rather than the secretary. He quit working at the factory and found a new job closer to home. His new boss was a Christian and attended the same church. As time passed, a man named Nicolae Matei became good friends with Nicu, helping him organize church programs and do mission work in the villages.

But life was never the same after that. Nicu was watched closely by the secret police, and the threat of imprisonment was always hanging over him. As the tension and pressure increased, Nicu and Monica prayed daily for protection, committing their lives to the God whose power alone could keep them safe.

13

Plans

Dazzling gold edged mounds of dark blue clouds in the western sky. Nicu shifted his position, straining to see over the heads of the people in front of him. People often waited in long lines for food from 3:00 in the morning until 7:00 at night. This particular line had been creeping along for almost half an hour. Would anything be left by the time he reached the front?

For the past two years, life in Romania had been growing increasingly difficult. Nicu wondered how much longer he would be able to provide for his family. But even more troubling was the oppressive shadow hanging over him in his church work. As he hurried homeward through the streets, loaf of bread in hand, Nicu looked up to the heavens. He had been fasting regularly and praying about their situation for months, searching for answers. As the husband and father in his home, he was responsible for the physical and spiritual wellbeing of his family. What did God want him to do?

When he opened the door, three-year-old Benjamin came running, excited about Tata being home from work. Swinging him up into his arms, Nicu carried him into the kitchen. Monica was working at the stove, smiling and cheerful as she prepared what little they had for the meal. No matter how scarce the provisions were, his dear wife never complained.

Little Daniel hung onto Monica's skirts, peeking around at Nicu with a dimpled grin. Daniel had celebrated his first birthday in March of 1978. He was healthy and perfectly formed, with brown hair and dark eyes. Nicu swung him up, holding his two small sons in both arms as he walked to the table. He sat down on a chair and took Daniel's hand, marveling at the tiny fingers curling around his big ones. How fragile and dependent these little ones were!

What did life hold for his children? Nicu wanted them to grow up with a happy childhood, but with the physical hardships and the dangers he faced with his church work, he wasn't sure it was possible. He brought up the subject later that night when he and Monica were in their room. "Are we doing what is best for our boys?"

She glanced up but didn't answer. They had discussed this before. Stepping over to the crib, Nicu looked down at his sleeping son. Daniel's lashes fanned his cheeks, and his soft brown hair glinted in the lamplight. "I wish I could give you something better than this constant uncertainty and stress."

She came to his side. "Have I complained?"

"Never," came his quick answer. "But I know it's been hard on you." He paused, debating his next words. "There's something I've been considering lately. As you know, many of my co-workers have left for Germany, hoping for a better life."

Monica took a slow breath, and he knew she realized where this was going. "Nicu Matei told me that he is planning to cross the border and go to Germany. He invited me to go with him, but I said I could not leave you with two small children." He paused, watching his wife relax, and then added, "Nicu is planning to come back later for his wife and daughter."

"He may never come back."

Monica's low words made him hesitate. The Romanian border was heavily patrolled with armed guards, and it was indeed dangerous to try to cross.

"But if he does, don't you think it's worth the risk for a better life?"

Nicu asked softly.

Her eyes met his. "Are you saying what I think you are?"

He nodded slowly, his gaze not leaving hers. "Monica, I'm considering this because I want what's best for *you*. You and the boys."

She looked away, gazing down at Daniel. "I would love to be free from all these pressures and be able to live a normal life with our boys . . ." She glanced up, a soft light in her eyes. "It would be wonderful. Would we go somewhere else after we get into Germany?"

"I would really like to go to America. They accept immigrants there, and we could have religious freedom. But we won't be able to go there directly. Perhaps we could go to Italy first. Or maybe to Belgrade, the capital city in Yugoslavia. I heard that the American embassy there helps people get to America. What do you think?"

"Well, my *tante* (aunt) Silvia lives in America, so we wouldn't be entirely lost if we'd go." Monica paused and then shook her head. "Are we actually thinking about leaving everything we've ever known for a foreign country?"

Nicu took her hand. "My dear, I've been thinking about this for a long time. But it's something we have to decide together. Are we willing to take the risk?"

She hesitated before meeting his gaze. "I'll support you in whatever you decide, Nicu. If it's God's will for us to go, I know He'll see us through."

Thundering breakers crashed in the distance, bringing foaming waves to shore. The sky was a dazzling blue, and a misty spray touched Nicu's face as he and Monica strolled along the beach. Benjamin and Daniel romped around them in the sand, stopping here and there to pick shells. "Are you happy?" he asked, smiling into Monica's eyes.

She beamed and slipped her hand into his. "It's wonderful here." It was the summer of 1979, and this was their first vacation together as a family.

They were all thoroughly enjoying it. They had traveled seven hundred kilometers by train to the Black Sea, where the pressures and tensions they faced at home seemed to fade away.

But this sense of freedom evaporated as soon as they returned home. In arranging his wife and daughter's escape a few months earlier, Nicu Matei had planned for his friend's escape at the same time. But Nicu had not been ready to leave then, so his information was given to a different guide who was to help them if they decided to escape. On their first Sunday at home from vacation, a brother in the church told Nicu and Monica that if they wanted to escape Romania, their guide was ready to help them. Matter-of-factly, the man told Nicu, "It's 50,000 lei per person, and everything has been arranged."

Nicu left church in a daze, his thoughts whirling. Now that the moment had come, it was harder than he had thought it would be. How could he leave the people he loved and the land he knew, not knowing if he would ever come back? And he had spent his savings the week before for their family vacation. It looked as though he would be forced to leave Monica and the boys behind for now, and he could scarcely bear the thought.

Nicu and Monica talked long into the night, facing together a storm of doubts, fears, and questions. Yet all they could do now was commit their lives into God's hands and trust Him to lead the way. If only they could take the sweet moments of love and laughter and togetherness in their numbered days and hold on to them! The time of separation would be upon them all too soon.

The family dressed in their Sunday best for a family picture the next day. *A farewell picture,* Monica thought. That evening Daniel lay sleeping in his crib while Nicu tucked Benjamin into bed in the other room. Was the love of her life leaving forever? She sank down on the bed and buried her face in both hands, giving way to the tears that had been threatening all day. The hours had flown by at an alarming pace, and she dreaded the morrow. It would be their last full day together.

Nicu found his wife kneeling beside the bed when he entered the room minutes later. They often prayed together, but seeing her there struck him to the heart. Slipping down beside Monica, he covered her hand with his and waited, praying silently.

At length she turned to him, her voice trembling with the depth of her emotions. "Nicu, I don't want you to go without me. On our wedding day I promised to follow you wherever you go. Please take me with you." Her voice was barely a whisper now. "If you're shot at the border, we'll all die together."

For a moment he could not speak. This beautiful young woman he loved was willing to risk her life for his sake. Reaching out, he grasped her shoulders. "All right, Monica. We'll ask the guide if it's possible for all of us to go. I borrowed 10,000 lei from a friend, and my brother gave 35,000 lei. I'll sell the furniture from our apartment to pay it all back. That adds up to only 45,000, and you know we need much more than that for the four of us. If the guide doesn't take it—" His grip tightened. "If he doesn't take it, we'll all go back. Whatever happens, we're in this together."

There was nothing but implicit trust and devotion in the soft hazel eyes that met his. "Do whatever you think is best, Nicu. I will follow you wherever you go."

"Nicu! It's good to see you!"

"And you, Tata." Nicu embraced his father, feeling a lump come into his throat. He had made a quick decision that morning to travel by train to the village where his parents lived, hoping to see them one last time before he left. Life had seemed surreal ever since Sunday—and yet it had a vivid clarity at the same time. Everything he saw held significance. The familiar homey living room, the homemade rug on the kitchen floor, the fresh bouquet of flowers on the table that Mama must have picked that morning—he was saying farewell to it all.

And yet his father had no idea of what was happening to him. This was the hardest, knowing he might never see Tata again. This man had raised him with a firm but loving hand, keeping in touch with him over the years. The words he had spoken to Nicu when he had left for boarding school years ago often came to his mind: "I can see in you a gift for becoming a leader in the church. But in the church there will always be problems. Don't forget—the dogs are barking, but the bear controls the road." How he would miss his dear *tata!*

And Mama wasn't at home, dashing any hopes of saying a silent goodbye to her. It was too dangerous to tell anyone, even his parents, that they were leaving the country. Nicu stayed as long as he could, chatting about the weather, the crops, his family—everything except the one thing so heavy on his heart.

When at last he rose to leave, Tata stood with him. "You must take some green beans and other things from the garden, son. I'll go out and—"

Nicu held up his hand. "Thanks, Tata, but I already have everything I need." He opened the door. "I want to walk to the fields where Ieremia is working before I catch the train." Giving his father one last hug, he stepped out, and they walked together to the gate.

On the street, Nicu paused to look back. Tata was still standing at the gate, watching him. He returned his son's wave before walking slowly back to the house. Nicu took a deep breath and squared his shoulders, turning away from his childhood home.

He found his brother working close to the road in the fields outside the village, sweat lining his brow. In the heat of the July day, the fields seemed to be blistering under the sun. "Nicu!" Ieremia straightened, whipping a handkerchief from his pocket to wipe his face. "What brings you here?"

"I came to visit." Nicu smiled and gestured toward the field. "Looks pretty dry out there. Think you'll have a good crop this year?"

"I hope so. We've been praying for rain." As they chatted, Nicu became aware of his brother's keen gaze. When they embraced in parting, Ieremia whispered, "You're escaping."

Nicu didn't answer. No words were needed. His brother knew.

The rumbling of the train wheels kept time with the questions weighing and sifting through his mind all the way home. *Are we doing the right thing?* He prayed for answers, for wisdom, for the assurance that his heavenly Father was leading him in this escape. By the time he reached his home, peace had stilled his heart. There was no turning back.

14

Escape

The family met with the guide that evening after Nicu returned home to make arrangements for the escape. A brother from the church was also there, planning to arrange an escape for himself and his nine-year-old son. They would be leaving the next night, and it was imperative to finalize their plans. Nicu tensed as the guide looked from him to his wife and sons. "Why are there four of you? I was planning on only one."

Monica straightened, her sweet young face resolute in the dim lighting. "We'll go with him, sir, or no one goes." Nicu smiled inside at her courage. No matter what, they were staying together.

The guide's brow furrowed. "It costs 50,000 lei for one person. Do you have enough for everyone?"

Nicu stepped forward. "All I have is 45,000 lei, sir. If it doesn't work, we'll go back."

The guide hesitated. He glanced at the other man, who stood waiting. Marcel met his gaze and spoke quietly. "I have only 50,000 lei for myself and my son. If it's not enough—"

The guide pursed his lips for a moment. Then he seemed to make up his mind. "It's not in order, but we'll do it." His gaze returned to Monica, lingering on the small boy in her arms. Monica stiffened, and Nicu's knees went weak.

"You can take the older boy, but the little one is not going along." The guide's voice left no room for argument. "He's too small to walk through mud, and he could cry at the border and give us all away."

Monica's face blanched, and she might have fallen if Nicu hadn't reached out to steady her. The guide's voice softened. "I'm sorry, but he cannot go."

Monica sat in the rocker, holding back tears that she knew would blind her vision as she studied her young son's face. Every detail of his smooth round cheeks, the shape of his eyes, the softness of his brown hair, was indelibly stamped upon her memory. Would she ever rock her baby again? Her arms tightened around him until she felt as if she could never let go. How dear, how precious, how unutterably sweet little Daniel was! How could she bear to leave him behind?

There was a soft footstep behind her, and her husband knelt silently beside the rocker. As he reached out to stroke Daniel's hair, his eyes filled with pain, Monica could hold back her tears no longer. As they came faster and faster, Nicu's arms went around her. She knew then that he was weeping too.

"I'll go see if Benjamin is ready." Setting aside his comb, Nicu glanced at his wife through the mirror. She was sitting on the bed, her gaze clinging to the face of the small boy in her arms. The anguish in her eyes made him swallow hard and turn away.

Stooping, he checked the bag they had packed for the escape. All they had to take along were the clothes they wore, pictures and school diplomas, his Bible, and a notebook with documents to prove his business. Dressed normally in hopes that people would think they were an ordinary family walking the streets, they planned to stop first at Monica's childhood home and leave Daniel there.

It was now almost 9:00 in the evening, and twilight was deepening into darkness. Nicu left the room, giving Monica a few minutes alone with her youngest son. Planting a kiss on Daniel's cheek, she pressed her face against his small, chubby one. She had determined that she would not cry tonight; she didn't want to look red and puffy when they visited her parents. But the resolution could not quiet the weeping in her heart.

Daniel patted her cheek and laughed, his dimples showing. The pain in Monica's mother-heart increased. *Oh, God, help me endure this!* Fighting against tears, she hurried from the room.

And then, much too soon, they were at the doorstep of Monica's parents' house. As Daniel put both little arms around his father's neck and hugged him tightly, Nicu felt his throat constrict. What were they doing to their son? Had they made the right decision?

It was all he could do to disengage those clinging arms and hand Daniel to his grandmother. "Take good care of him."

"Oh, we will!" Ana Bejenaru said in a fervent whisper. Her eyes held love, pain, and fear all at once.

As he closed the door, Nicu saw that all the color had fled from his wife's face, and her lips were tight and drawn. He stepped close to her and squeezed her hand. In a hoarse whisper, he said, "He *will* be all right." Then he lifted Benjamin into his arms and led the way into the street.

They traveled silently through the night—a group of six, moving swiftly through swampy fields, hearts pounding with fear. At any moment the call could come, ending their journey and sending them back to an even worse life than the one they were trying to escape. The penalty for escape was prison—or worse.

The guide went first, leading the way. Nicu walked next in line, carrying Benjamin. He had given the four-year-old a pill so he would sleep, and the small boy was sleeping now against his shoulder. Monica followed close behind, with Marcel and his son Christian bringing up the rear. The night was warm, with a mild breeze and singing crickets. Stars shone high above. It would have been a beautiful night if anyone had noticed. But the twenty-two kilometers to the river seemed endless. Up one hill and down another, stumbling over unfamiliar ruts in the ground, mud splattering their clothes as they waded through it. At last they stood on the shores of the river, where moonlight was cresting the waves with silver-blue sparkles.

"I'll go first and see how deep it is," the guide whispered. "The rest of you wait here." The tense group on shore strained to see as his dark figure moved deeper and deeper into the water. Long black shadows soon hid him from sight. Would he make it through all right? They couldn't see or hear anything except the gentle murmur of the river.

Just as Nicu was beginning to wonder if the guide would return, he appeared again, wading to shore. "We can make it easily," he assured them. "The water is only chest-deep." Taking Nicu's bag, he plunged back into the water. One by one they followed—Nicu with Benjamin, Monica, Marcel, and Christian. As the water became deeper, it swirled around them, slowing their progress. They struggled on toward the distant shore, keeping their course until at last the river bed rose again into shallower water.

"Be very careful here," the guide warned as they reached the shore. "The border is in about two and a half meters. It's a fine sand, with two wires that we must step across. If we touch them, rockets will go off and the guards will know that someone is here."

The wires were about three meters apart. Nicu followed the guide, cautious to steer clear of the wires. He watched with bated breath as the others stepped across, one by one. At last they were all safely across the border and ready to move on.

Then they heard it.

Woof! Woof! The deep barking of dogs shattered the still night air, making everyone freeze in their tracks. "Military dogs," the guide whispered, and

ESCAPE

Nicu knew they had reason to be afraid. He jumped as the first rockets shot up into the night sky, brightening it with a white glow. Monica gasped and clutched his arm. The guards shot rockets again, searching for whatever had alarmed the dogs. They stood still, waiting in terrified suspense. At last the barking ceased, and the night became quiet again.

Only then did they dare to move on into the forest. As the path wove through the trees, the darkness grew so intense that Nicu could not even see his finger in front of his face. He listened closely to the guide's footsteps in front of him, keeping tight hold of the small boy in his arms. Would this jolting gait cause Benjamin to wake up and ask, "Tata, when will we get there?" Would a branch strike him and make him cry? Nicu shuddered and sent a silent prayer heavenward—something he had been doing all night as they traveled. He didn't even want to think about what could happen if Benjamin woke up.

The guide stopped abruptly. Rockets were shooting skyward again, their white glow illuminating the forest. How Nicu longed for this to be over! They stood still, listening intently as the night grew silent once more. The danger wasn't over, but they could go on. Why, then, wasn't the guide moving ahead?

"I don't know where we are," the guide's whisper came through the darkness. "I think we should go back."

Go back? Nicu stared, wishing he could see the guide's face. After all this way, go back through the dark forest? Back across the border? Across the river? He tensed, and there was a note of finality in his quiet tone when he spoke. "No. We'll go forward." Without waiting for an answer, he started walking again. Monica followed close behind, and after a surprised moment the others fell into line.

In charge of the group now, Nicu led the way deeper into the forest. The path led up and up until sudden moonlight broke through the darkness. Before them lay an open field, and they were standing at the edge of the forest. The guide stepped up beside him, looking around with an air of relief.

"Now I know where I am," he said. "Let's go in this direction." Once again he led the way, with the others following. This ground was rocky, and Nicu felt relieved that there was no fine sand on the rocks to leave behind footprints.

Ahead, a towering shape appeared in the darkness. Nicu's eyes widened. They were heading straight toward a guard house! It was built two meters off the ground and supported with posts, with a ladder reaching to the top. Quickening his pace, he moved up beside the guide. "Why are we going there?" he whispered. "That's the guard house."

The guide turned his head. "There isn't anyone there. It's just something to scare the people who come through here."

Nicu said nothing more. This guide knew what he was doing; he could trust him. Who was he, anyway? He had told them his name, but they knew it was likely not his real name. Was he a brother in the faith? It was better not to know. If they were caught, his ignorance would protect this man who was leading them to freedom.

"I will leave you now and go back," the guide was saying. "This rocky place is the border of Yugoslavia."

But Nicu found it hard to believe him. "How do I know I'm in Yugoslavia?"

The guide stood still for a moment, thinking. It was 5:00 in the morning, and dawn was another hour away. "All right," he said at length. "I'll stay with you until you're sure of where you are." They walked until dawn's first light was streaking the sky, stopping when they heard voices ahead. "Let me go forward and listen," Nicu offered. "I know the Yugoslavian language."

Still carrying Benjamin, he went in the direction of the voices and listened. What language were they speaking? Then he recognized the language of the Serbs, a people group from Yugoslavia.

"They are Serbs," Nicu told the others when he returned. He glanced at the guide and smiled. "I know now that we're in Yugoslavia, sir. You can go back." Reaching out, he shook his hand. "Thank you for everything you've done for us."

Monica nodded, her face pale and tired in the early morning dawn. But she managed a smile. "Yes, thank you so much."

Marcel and Christian echoed their thanks, and Nicu led a word of prayer as they stood together. "Dear Lord, we praise you for protecting us and giving us a safe journey so far. Bless our guide for his willingness to help us, and protect him as he goes back to Romania. In Jesus' name I pray. Amen."

With a quick smile the guide was gone, slipping silently back the way they had come.

15

Caught!

Unable to go any farther, the group rested in the field. Rocky ground didn't offer the most comfortable places for rest, but they were too tired to care. As the light grew brighter, birds twittered softly in the trees and creamy coral tinted the eastern sky, giving the morning an ethereal beauty.

But they still hadn't reached freedom. As Nicu dozed, images of the river, mud, barking dogs, and rockets danced through his brain. He awoke with a start when Benjamin stirred on the ground next to him. After carrying the small boy for nine hours straight, Nicu had been thankful to lay him down and rest his weary arms. Now Benjamin sat up slowly, his wide brown eyes looking around with wonder.

"Benny?" Reaching out, Nicu stroked his son's hair. "I'm right here," he said softly. "And Mama's here too."

"Where are we?" Benjamin asked.

Beside Nicu, Monica leaned forward. "We're in Yugoslavia, son." She hesitated, and a pensive look came into her eyes. "I wonder how Daniel is this morning. Did he cry last night at bedtime? Is he . . ." Her voice broke and a tear slid down her cheek.

Nicu had also often thought of the son they had left behind while traveling through the long night. No doubt these questions would haunt them daily in the weeks to come. But all they could do was leave Daniel in God's hands.

Standing up, he held out his hands to Monica. "Come," he said softly. "We must go."

They walked in the direction of the voices Nicu had heard earlier, entering a road that led toward the distant city. Two soldiers came toward them, standing at attention as they questioned the small, weary group of travelers. "Who are you?"

"We have come from Romania," Nicu responded.

The soldiers weren't satisfied with his answer. "Did you cross the border legally?"

Nicu hesitated. "No."

They were taken directly to the police station, where a meal was served. Nicu saw the relief in his wife's eyes and smiled. The police certainly treated them better here than in Romania. Perhaps things would go well for them after all.

Minutes later he wasn't so sure. "You will serve time in prison for crossing the border illegally." As the officer spoke, Nicu felt the air leave his lungs. After all they had gone through, had it actually come to this?

"You and the other man who escaped with you will be taken to prison." As though from far away, he heard the officer's voice still speaking. "Your wife and the children will be sent elsewhere. You are dismissed."

Nicu's feet felt like lead as he moved through the door to where the guard was waiting.

He was placed in a cell with two other prisoners. Built with stone walls, a low, sloping ceiling and no windows, the room was under a stairway. Nicu tossed and turned on the hard cot, unable to sleep. *Where are my wife and Benjamin? What is happening to them? Will I ever see them again?* The questions pounded through his brain—haunting, relentless questions, all answered with a silence that seemed to mock his pain.

Two long days crept by. "Where did you come from? How did you cross the border? Why did you escape? Who helped you? How much did you pay?" The Yugoslavian police spoke in Romanian, hurling the questions at him in rapid succession. Nicu skirted the truth as much as he dared, avoiding giving any names. He was surprised at how much these officers knew about him.

"What would you say if we sent you back to Romania?" one of the officers asked, leaning forward across the desk. Dressed in plain clothes, he looked as though he belonged to the secret police.

The color drained from Nicu's face. Go back to Romania and suffer vengeful beatings at the hands of the police who often killed or paralyzed their victims? He met the officer's gaze. "I pray you, don't send me back to Romania! They would treat me in such a way that I would not be a normal person anymore."

The officer looked at him keenly. "Your mother was sent here to convince you to go back to Romania. I told her not to worry about you; that it's going well with you and your wife. I told her you didn't want to go back."

Nicu made no answer. He would have loved to see his dear mama again, but it was out of the question. Squaring his shoulders, he spoke quietly. "How is my wife?"

"Everything is okay with her," the officer answered.

The answer did not satisfy him, but the officer would say nothing more.

The prison schedule was rigid, with only a daily walk allowed around the prison yard under the escort of a guard. Nicu turned his face toward the sunlight, taking a deep breath of fresh air. This was the second day he had been in prison, and it felt good to relax a little. It was stressful to be in a cell all day long with a Serb who had killed his mother and an Italian who had killed a four-year-old girl in an accident.

Nicu glanced around and then straightened abruptly. In the distance he could see Marcel walking in another part of the prison yard! How good it was to see his friend. If only they could speak to each other. He smiled across the yard to Marcel, and Marcel smiled back.

Then Nicu froze, staring in horror. The prisoners were finished with their walk now, and the guards were ordering them back to their rooms. But there was trouble across the yard. The guard must have seen Marcel smile, for he had raised his rubber club and was bringing it down over his head as hard as he could.

Nicu saw Marcel instinctively duck, and the club hit the back of his head. His friend said nothing; he simply walked on. But the scene was burned into Nicu's mind as he filed into prison with the others. Did that guard have no heart? How long would they have to endure this?

By the third day, Nicu had a throbbing headache. Knocking on the door, he asked the guard to open it. First he explained about his headache, and then said slowly, "I'll answer your questions directly now. I was persecuted in Romania for being a Christian, and I wanted to leave the country together with my family. I risked my life crossing the border." He lifted his aching head with effort. "Please, if it's possible, help me to get to America somehow. I heard that if I would be able to get to Belgrade, I could go to the American embassy and get help."

The guard stood silently, his face unreadable in the shadowy grayness of the stone walls. "Wait here," he said gruffly at length. Without another word he closed the door, and Nicu heard the grate of keys in the lock.

Stepping back to the hard cot, he knelt and prayed.

Three hours passed before the guard came back. "Do you still have a headache?" he asked.

Nicu felt a little amused at the ironic question. Did they think he had something else to report? "No, I don't have a headache anymore."

The guard handed him a piece of bread and closed the door. As he sat down again, Nicu turned the hard, coarse bread over in his hands. This was often what they were served for a meal, but the meager fare didn't bother him. He was used to spending a lot of time in fasting and prayer, and these days he hardly had any appetite.

Where are my wife and son? What is happening to them? Once more the questions haunted him long into the night.

16

Where Is God?

Laughing and shouting, Benjamin raced down the path with Christian, chasing a squirrel. From her place on the park bench, Monica smiled as she watched the boys. It was good to see them happy. If only Nicu and Marcel could be with them! Monica and Nicu had been questioned separately by the police and torn apart with no assurance of ever seeing each other again. She and the boys had been taken to the home of a retired policeman, where they were kept under constant supervision. They were never allowed to be alone, even during their daily walks in the park. The retired policeman wasn't taking any chances of them fleeing.

It could be worse, Monica reflected. The man and his wife were friendly to her and the boys, and the park provided a pleasant place to walk with its shady trees and colorful flowers. But of course, she could hardly enjoy it in the face of the unknowns. Tears filled her eyes and she brushed them quickly away, not wanting her escort to notice. What was happening to her husband in prison? Was he doing all right? Would she ever see him again?

Her thoughts flew homeward, back to the city of Timișoara where they had left family and friends; back to the small child they had left behind. How her arms ached to hold her toddler! The heartache of leaving Daniel, and now Nicu, was so sharp that it almost caused physical pain. *Will the four of us ever be together again?*

"Mama!" Benjamin was running toward her, his brown hair shining in the sun, his eyes sparkling. "I picked this flower for you!"

"Oh, Benny, it's beautiful! Thank you." Monica took the flaming red poppy from his hand, careful not to harm the fragile petals. Tears came again to her eyes, but this time she did not brush them away. Somehow the flower reminded her that even here in this lonely place, God had not forsaken her. His love was aglow in the vibrant beauty of the scarlet poppy.

Nicu balanced on the edge of the hard cot, watching as his friend Marcel set aside his empty plate. "They always make sure we don't get enough," Marcel said ruefully.

"But I'm never hungry these days," Nicu admitted. He glanced around the room. After the first three days of interrogation, he had been placed in the same cell as Marcel. But with thirty other men in the same room, they were seldom alone. He lowered his voice. "These conditions are deplorable!"

Marcel gave a silent nod. From the open toilet chair in the far corner to the small window in the door where they received their meals, they had no privacy at all. Nicu had been appointed chief over the cell, in which he had to report the number of prisoners every morning. This was now the fifth day of his imprisonment, and it felt as though an eternity had passed since he had seen his wife and children.

Nicu still asked about Monica and Benjamin every chance he had. Always he received the same answer: "Everything is okay." But somehow, he could not shake off the uneasy feeling that everything was *not* okay with his dear wife. Yet there was nothing he could do except pray and trust God to keep His protecting hand over her.

Monica awoke with a start. The room where she slept with the boys was lit faintly by moonbeams shining through the drapes. The deep, even breathing of the boys across the room told her they were still asleep. What had awakened her? She lay still, listening intently.

There it was again—the unmistakable sound of her door creeping open stealthily. Her whole body stiffened with terror. She recognized that heavy tread. Why was the retired policeman coming into her room?

The man came nearer until he was standing beside her bed. Monica decided to pretend to be asleep, but she could scarcely hold back a scream when she felt his hand touch her. Her brain spun wildly for a few seconds, wondering if there was anything she could do. But then the man withdrew his hand. Monica heard him turn and step quietly out of the room.

Even though the door closed behind the man, Monica felt thoroughly shaken. This man was terribly bold! Why had God brought her here, knowing the danger she would be in? She had never experienced anything like this before. Oh, how she longed to leave this horrible place and be with her husband again!

After that night, Monica always made certain she piled furniture in front of the door to keep the man from entering. She was thankful when his friendliness toward her cooled, but as the long days dragged by, an oppressive cloud descended over her spirit. She longed to give her fears to God—to believe that He made no mistakes. But she was beginning to wonder if she would ever see Nicu again.

The officers were unable to find anything against Nicu and Marcel. After ten days of imprisonment, they were released and taken to a refugee camp in a town near Belgrade, the capital city of Yugoslavia. There they were crammed into a room with sixty-five other refugees, their eyes filled with despair and their faces hollow from hunger. Nicu made no effort to join the crowd that rushed like animals to the big pot of food whenever a meal was served. He knew that whoever was left could not get any, but he continued to have little appetite.

The night they had escaped seemed like a lifetime ago. The only ray of light in this dark place was the knowledge that he wasn't going to be sent back to Romania. Beyond that, he had no idea what the future held. He was persistent in asking if it was possible to see his wife and child, but still he received no satisfactory answers.

Deep depression began to shroud Nicu. At night, sleep eluded him, and his anguished prayers seemed to reach no farther than the ceiling. "God, what have I done? Why am I here?" Every sinful thought, word, and deed he had committed against the Almighty played out like a film before him—taunting, mocking, scorning. Hot tears scalded his eyes as he repented in brokenness of spirit, crying out to God for mercy and forgiveness. He pleaded for one more chance to see his wife and son. The heavy burden on his heart seemed to be crushing him slowly, destroying his peace and will to live.

By the fifth morning at the camp, Nicu felt that his nerves were ready to snap. Emotionally spent and exhausted, he hardly even heard the familiar commotion of refugees rushing to grab what they could from the big pot of food on the floor. Instead, he stared out the window as pale light stole across the land. When was all this going to be over?

Only when he felt a hand on his shoulder did he look up. "Nicu, I brought you something to eat." Marcel was standing there, watching him with concern. "Are you all right?"

Nicu shook his head. His hands trembled as he took the plate from his friend. "It's eighteen days now since I've been separated from my wife and son, Marcel," he said hoarsely. "Eighteen."

Marcel's grip tightened. He knew all too well how separation felt. Not only was he separated from his son, but he had also left his wife in Romania for the time being. "Take heart, my friend," he said. "I found out this morning that we're going to be released from this refugee camp and taken to a hotel in Belgrade. It's a hotel for refugees, and we'll be free."

Hope leaped into Nicu's eyes. "Will we meet Monica and the boys there?"

"I don't know, but I hope so." Marcel took a deep breath. "I'm as eager to see my son again as you are to see your wife and child. It seems like it's been . . ."

"Forever," Nicu supplied fervently.

Marcel smiled a little. "Almost." He took a bite of the thin soup. "If they aren't at the hotel, we'll search for them."

Nicu looked down, his hands trembling again. "Marcel, I won't be able to rest until I know where they are and that they are safe."

Before they were released that afternoon, Nicu and Marcel were told that Monica and the boys were indeed waiting for them at the hotel. Time could hardly go fast enough after that.

17

Together Again

When they were brought to the hotel in Belgrade, Monica felt as if a huge burden had rolled off her shoulders. She stood at the window, watching the street while the boys explored the room. How thankful she was to be away from the retired policeman's home! Here at the hotel they were free—free to live as they pleased without supervision, free to walk and run and roam at will.

And Nicu would be coming to meet them here! She could hardly wait to see him again. The eighteen days of their separation had seemed like an eternity.

Monica straightened abruptly as a knock came on the door. Her heart leaped. Could this be the moment she was waiting for? Benjamin came running and she took his hand, keeping him close to her as she opened the door.

Two men stood on the landing outside. One was shorter than the other, his smile and his brown hair shining in the sunlight. It was her husband. Monica's vision suddenly blurred.

"Monica!" Nicu stepped toward her with open arms, and she fell into them without a word. The boys barreled through the door behind her, turning the landing into a jubilant meeting place.

After being apart for so many days, Nicu and Monica's joy in being together again knew no bounds. They were only vaguely aware of the happy reunion between Marcel and his son nearby. Nicu scooped up Benjamin with one arm, keeping the other around his wife. "You both look wonderful," he said, beaming.

Monica laughed shakily through her tears. "So do you, dear, though you look thinner since I last saw you." She rested her head against his shoulder. "Oh, Nicu, I can't tell you how much I've missed you!"

"And I you, Monica. Every day I wondered what was happening with my wife and son. I didn't know if I would ever see you again." Nicu stopped, unable to go on.

"Tata? Mama?" Benjamin looked from one to the other, his face worried. "What's wrong?"

"We're happy, son, that's all." Nicu cleared his throat and ruffled Benjamin's hair. "Were you a good boy for Mama while I was gone?"

"Oh, yes!" Benjamin beamed. "I picked a poppy for her in the park."

"The park?"

"We were allowed to walk there every day." Monica paused, and Nicu saw a shadow darken her eyes. Concern swept over him anew. What had happened to his beloved wife during his absence?

He drew her close again. "We have a lot to catch up on, dearest. But first, let's go inside and thank the Lord for bringing us back together."

"We have so much to thank Him for," she said softly, her eyes shining again.

The sky seemed bluer, the trees greener, and the flowers brighter that afternoon as they walked hand in hand down the street. Benjamin ran ahead, looking back every few minutes to make sure his parents were still following. Divine protection had kept them in the past few weeks, and though they missed their precious younger son, they reveled in being together again.

"At least I feel more human since we washed our clothes," Nicu said, grinning at Monica. "These are all I had to wear, and after eighteen days they were filthy! But I feel a lot better."

"I just wish I could have had soap to wash them with," Monica said.

"And if we'd only have money, we could buy something to eat here at the marketplace," Nicu added. They were entering the city square, where tables were set up with clerks selling their wares. Benjamin was already hovering over a table filled with fruits. The sweet scents were mouthwatering—grapes, apples, bananas, and strawberries. Nicu couldn't resist searching his pockets, though he knew they were empty. "Nothing," he said finally in despair.

Monica smiled. "Don't worry about it. Someday we'll have money again to buy wonderful fruit like this. At least we can get a free meal at the hotel."

"We should go back," Nicu said, glancing at his watch. "It's almost time for the evening meal." He raised his voice. "Come, Benny! It's time to go."

"Will Christian be there?" Benjamin raced back to them and caught Nicu's hand.

Nicu tousled his hair affectionately. "I suppose he will be. You like Christian, don't you?"

"They played together a lot while you were gone," Monica said. "Christian was really good with Benjamin."

They sat together with Marcel and Christian for supper at the hotel. "I want to go to the German embassy tomorrow," Marcel told them. "I'm going to ask for help to get to Germany. It shouldn't be too hard for me to get there, since I have German ethnicity." He looked questioningly at the young couple across from him. "Are you still thinking you'll go to America?"

Nicu nodded. "We'd like to."

"Why don't you come to Germany and go to America from there?" Marcel asked. "It's possible to do that."

"Really?" Nicu glanced at Monica. "We'll have to consider it."

At Marcel's invitation they accompanied their friends to the German embassy the next morning. Marcel went inside to make his request. When he came out, he said cheerfully, "They gave me a train ticket, money, and food to go to a refugee camp in Nuremberg, Germany. We have to leave Yugoslavia in forty-eight hours."

"You're going to a refugee camp?"

Marcel winced a little at Nicu's question. "Maybe this one will be different."

Nicu fell silent. *Now he's leaving; what will we do?* It had been so quick and easy for his friend to receive help. Could they receive the same help?

"Marcel, you said that in Germany we can still go to America if we want to," he said at length. "Would you return with us to the German embassy tomorrow and ask them if they'll help us too?"

"Of course I will," Marcel answered immediately. "You helped me cross the border, and I'm glad to help you in any way I can."

Accordingly, they all went to the embassy again the next morning. The German secretary behind the desk stood up, a smile lighting her blue eyes as she looked at Nicu's little family. "I'll go to the ambassador and ask if we can help you," she said through Marcel's interpretation. With another smile, she disappeared through the door.

Nicu lost count of how many times he checked his watch during the next hour. Still they waited as the minutes dragged on. Thirty minutes passed, then forty, before the secretary finally appeared again. "The ambassador said we'll help you if the UN gives permission," she said, sitting down at her desk. "I've made the call, and now we're waiting for an answer."

Knowing they were already registered as refugees under the United Nations, Nicu felt his hopes rise. But they had to wait another hour before they finally received their answer. "The UN said that if it's easy for us to help you and we want to, we can go ahead," the secretary told them at last. "If you wait here, we'll help you."

It was afternoon when they finally walked back to the hotel with new passports, along with train tickets, money, and food. Nicu looked up into the hazy blue sky, feeling better than he had since the escape. Though their future was still uncertain, he took comfort in knowing that God was leading them and they were together.

18

The Promise

They heard the train's whistle minutes before it rumbled into the station where they were waiting. "We'll go through Austria and Hungary to get to Germany," Marcel explained as they settled into their seats. "Have your passports ready when we stop at the borders."

The train track wove through both urban and country landscapes, with snow-peaked mountains forming distant ranges along the horizon. At the borders they were searched, with their IDs and documents recorded. It was 11:00 a.m. when they finally arrived at the Nuremberg station in Germany.

"Do you know how to get to the refugee camp from here?" Nicu asked Marcel as they walked out of the station.

"I have directions, but it'll probably take me some time to find it. What are you planning to do?"

"Well, I have a phone number to call. Nicu Matei—he escaped from Romania last year and went to America, you know—also helped his brother Abraham get to Germany. Abraham lives about two hours away from here in Munich. I'll call him as soon as I get to a phone booth; but if this doesn't work out, I don't know what we're going to do."

"I'll wait with you until you find out," Marcel offered.

"Thanks," Nicu said gratefully. "We weren't ready to be on our own in this strange place. You know this country better than we do."

Abraham answered on the second ring. "Stay at the station," he said when Nicu explained their situation. "I'm coming."

"It seems like we've been doing a lot of waiting these past few days," Monica said as they sat down on a bench.

"At least we're waiting together." Nicu smiled at her and set Benjamin on his knee. "I'm not sure how Abraham is going to help us, though. He's in school trying to learn German because he wants to become a doctor, and he doesn't really have a place of his own. But I'm sure something will work out," he added. "God has never failed us yet."

Abraham was a tall man with thinning hair and a wide smile. He took them to the home of a family from the church he attended. "It's perfect," the couple told Abraham. "We were planning to leave on a two-week vacation. They can live here during the two weeks we're gone and look after the house for us."

"They're trusting us with a lot," Nicu said dubiously when Abraham relayed the message to him.

Abraham laughed. "And that's not all. They said you can help yourself to anything you need—food in the refrigerator, or whatever. You can also take care of their animals."

"Tell them we'll gladly do it," Nicu responded. "We appreciate all they're doing for us."

He and Monica shook hands with the couple and then walked outside with Abraham. "I'll look for a place for you to stay while you're living here," Abraham said, opening his car door. "I may not be able to find much, but I'll see what I can do."

Reaching out, Nicu gripped his hand. "Thanks for everything, friend. I don't know what we'd do if you weren't here to help us."

From where she stood at the ironing board, Monica could feel a gentle breeze drifting in through the open window. Outside, Nicu was heading toward the chicken coop with Benjamin at his side, whistling a cheery tune. They had already fed the rabbits. She smiled and turned back to her ironing. She had done some cleaning earlier, wanting to do her part in expressing appreciation to this family who had so kindly offered their home for two weeks.

Deciding not to go to the refugee camp, Marcel and Christian were also staying with them. They had gone through so much together, and it was good to be with friends. On Sunday they attended Abraham's church. Though they couldn't understand the German service, it lifted their spirits to recognize the familiar tune of "What a Friend We Have in Jesus." What a precious reminder that God understood how their hearts ached for Daniel, and that He promised to bear their sorrows! What a privilege to be able to carry their unknown future to the Lord and trust Him to guide them! Monica felt more peaceful now than she had since they had left Romania.

She served coffee on the porch that evening as the sun slipped toward the western hills. "Abraham told me today that he found an apartment for us," Nicu said, wrapping his hands around the warm mug.

"He's just in time," Marcel commented. "The family is coming back tomorrow."

Monica sat down beside Nicu on the swing. "How big is the apartment?"

"He said it's very small. It used to be an attic, and no one has lived there for five years." Nicu took a sip of coffee, his eyes thoughtful. "We're starting all over again. We have no money, we don't know the language—"

"But we have the Lord and each other," Monica reminded him.

"God has been good to us." Nicu turned back to Marcel and smiled. "When we move to the apartment, you and Christian are welcome to live there with us."

"You mean that?" Marcel stared from Nicu to Monica, who nodded and smiled.

"You have helped us so much," she said softly. "Now we want to help you."

After the others had gone to bed, Nicu and Monica lingered together on the porch swing, watching stars appear in the night sky. "I've been asking around about how we can get Daniel," Nicu confided. "They tell me that we can bring him here through the Red Cross."

Monica's heart leaped. "Oh, I hope so," she breathed, tears misting her eyes. "I have no doubt that my parents love Daniel and treat him as their own, but every day I long to see him and hold him."

Nicu slipped an arm around her shoulders. "So do I, dear. We'll go to the office of the International Red Cross as soon as possible and ask them to help us."

Monica's eyes clouded. "I'm almost afraid to hope. Nicu, we were under so much stress with your church work before we escaped. Then we were separated for eighteen days after we crossed the border. Is God trying to show us something in all the pain and separation we've been through?"

He sat deep in thought. "It may be a test of our faith," he said at length. "Perhaps God is preparing us for something."

"But what could it be?"

He shook his head. "I don't know. We can only trust that though we don't understand what is happening in our lives, God knows what He's doing and makes no mistakes."

Nicu shifted his position on the chair, glancing at his watch. The ten minutes he had been waiting to speak to the representative at the American embassy felt like twenty. Would his family stay in Germany or go to America?

They were living in the apartment now, and Nicu knew a decision needed to be made. He planned to apply for political asylum in both Germany and America. If Germany did not grant his family citizenship, they would have to go back to Romania—unless America would take them in. Nicu had his requests carefully thought out. He had two invitations to show the embassy—the first one was from Monica's *tante* Silvia, who lived in Detroit, Michigan. A pastor from a large church in America had also sent an invitation, offering to support them until they could make a living of their own. He had high hopes that they would be able go.

But the weeks went by, and they heard nothing. On Sunday at church, as he listened to the choir singing, Nicu felt his courage rise. Though he couldn't understand all the German words, the tune of "Amazing Grace" was familiar. God's grace was indeed sufficient to carry them through.

After the service, Nicu shook hands with the pastor. "Peace be with you," he said.

The pastor of the German church spoke Romanian. He smiled. "Brother Nicu, how have you been doing?"

"The Lord has blessed us," Nicu answered. "We're settled in our apartment now and thankful to have a roof over our heads." He grinned. "Everything about it is small—a small bedroom, living room, kitchen, bathroom, and a small hall that we use as another bedroom. My wife is kept busy cooking and cleaning for the five people who occupy it. But we're grateful for a roof over our heads!"

"Both you and Marcel have jobs, yes?"

Nicu nodded. "The income is low, but it's better than nothing. Marcel and I divide the rent, and Marcel helps provide our meals."

"It's amazing how God has led you and kept you," the pastor commented. "Your story shows that God's grace is sufficient even in the darkest times."

Nicu met his gaze. "That's just what I was thinking, pastor. After I got out of prison, I told my wife that a person who doesn't believe in Christ would not dare get into prison. It would be impossible for him to think and be able to answer what they ask there."

The pastor's eyes were sober. "There are always people who will want to hurt us, but we don't need to fear them." His brow knit thoughtfully. "Isn't there a text in Revelation that talks about that?" He paged through his Bible. "Ah, yes, here it is—Revelation 2:10. 'Fear none of those things which thou shalt suffer: behold, the devil shall cast some of you into prison, that ye may be tried; and ye shall have tribulation ten days: be thou faithful unto death, and I will give thee a crown of life.' "

Nicu reflected on the words and looked up at the pastor. "Thank you for sharing this with me," he said quietly. "It is indeed a blessed promise."

19

"Please Help Us Bring Our Son"

Snow drifted down to the streets, reflecting the streetlights. Icicles hung from the tiled roofs of shops and houses as Marcel and Nicu walked together, deep in conversation. Their paths had crossed while coming home from work, and the apartment was only a block away.

"I've been trying to save money to bring my wife to Romania," Marcel was saying. "I appreciate all you've done for Christian and me, but I can't wait for my wife to join us here and be able to move into a home of our own."

Nicu gave his friend an empathetic glance. "We went to the Red Cross and asked them to help bring Daniel here. But they said they couldn't help us until we have German citizenship. They said, 'Come to our office once you are German citizens.'" Nicu stopped. It pained him to remember how sad and helpless they had felt.

"What are you planning to do?" Marcel asked.

Nicu straightened his shoulders. "We've decided to write separate letters to Nicolae Ceaușescu and his wife and ask them for help in bringing our son here."

Marcel's eyes widened. "You're going to write to the president of Romania?"

"He and his wife are both very powerful. Maybe they'll find it in their hearts to help us."

"Maybe." Marcel sounded doubtful, but Nicu's mind was made up. He and Monica were desperate for their son. They had to do something.

Nicu renewed his resolve that night as he watched Benjamin break his cookie in half, placing the bigger half beside his plate. "This is for Daniel when he comes," he said, and the look in his eyes made Nicu's throat tighten. Benjamin always saved half of his food for his little brother who was missing.

Pushing back his chair from the table, Nicu strode to his desk. As he clicked his pen, he glanced at the calendar: December 16, 1979. It had been four months since they had left Romania—four long, long months since he had last seen his youngest son. With a quick, steady hand, Nicu wrote the letters and slid them into separate envelopes. He would mail them to the president and his wife first thing in the morning and wait on God for the answer.

Day after day they waited. One week. Two weeks. Three weeks. There was no answer. They wrote a letter to the Romanian embassy in Germany and waited again. Two more agonizing weeks dragged by.

"We can't go on like this any longer," Nicu said by the end of the second week. He looked into Monica's eyes in the semi-darkness of their tiny room, his hand firm on her shoulder. "I'm going to cross the border illegally back into Romania and bring our son back."

"What?" She gasped, and her face paled.

"What else can we do, Monica?" His voice was low with intensity. "There's no answer from anywhere. I'm willing to take the risk!"

"It's just too dangerous, dear." A tremor passed through her frame, echoing in her words. "I could lose both of you!"

Nicu knew she was right. He was silent for a long moment, thinking. "Okay," he said at last. "I know of only one more thing to try. Tomorrow I'll visit the Romanian embassy here in Germany and ask them for help."

But he hit a wall there as well. "My wife and I have two sons," he told the secretary. "One son is with us here in Germany, and the little one is

"PLEASE HELP US BRING OUR SON"

still in Romania. He's part of our family."

"Write down your request and I'll put it in your file," she said, looking bored as she thumbed through the stack of files on her desk. No doubt she received many requests like this one. Germany held many Romanian refugees. "The embassy will have an answer for you soon."

But the days turned into weeks, and they heard nothing.

"It's a toddler, two years old, and I need help getting him to his parents."

Pavel Craiovan spoke the words over and over as he went to one Romanian official after another, asking for help to take his nephew to Germany. Even when he was pushed out one door, he always opened another, insisting that he needed help to get a two-year-old back to his parents. He could only imagine what his brother and sister-in-law were going through, starting over in a strange country without their youngest son. If possible, he would get a passport for both himself and Daniel and take him to them by plane.

Pavel was finally able to get a passport for Daniel, but not for himself. Someone else with a passport would have to take his nephew to Germany—someone he could trust to protect the baby and keep him safe. But who?

"I have family in Germany," a colleague said when he explained the situation at work. "Perhaps I could take him." There was a sparkle in the lady's eyes that Pavel couldn't help noticing. Lili was a kind lady from a well-to-do family. With her gentle ways, it likely wouldn't take her long to befriend Daniel.

What shall I do, Lord? Pavel sent a silent prayer heavenward as he pondered the situation. At length he straightened and met Lili's gaze. "If you promise to take good care of him, I'll make the arrangements."

She smiled. "I love children, Pavel. After we learn to know each other, I'm sure your nephew and I will get along fine."

Pavel was able to write to Nicu and Monica and tell them the arrangements. On the February morning that they were scheduled to leave for the airport, Pavel met Lili and her family with Daniel in his arms. "This lady will take you to your mama and *tata*," he said to his nephew.

Daniel's face lit up. As they drove to the airport, he became acquainted with Lili. When the time came to board the plane, Daniel took Lili's hand without hesitation and walked confidently with her family through the airport to the terminal gate. Pavel stood watching until they vanished from sight, returning Daniel's wave when he looked back. The boy's grandparents had shed tears when he left their home, and Pavel knew that many of the relatives would also miss Daniel. But the small boy belonged with his own family.

Daniel quickly became a favorite with Lili's family, chattering happily about many things as they walked through the Frankfurt airport. He could scarcely contain his excitement when they reached the door, where they had to wait for a few minutes before being allowed to go out to the welcoming crowd. Beaming friends were waiting with Nicu and Monica for their son, making it a large group.

Placing a hand on Daniel's shoulder, Lili leaned down to talk to him. "Which one is your *tata*?"

Looking out across the crowd, Daniel didn't answer for a moment. Then his grin spread from ear to ear as he pointed to a somewhat shorter-than-average young man standing near the front. "That one is!"

Lili's eyes twinkled. "Oh, he looks like a boy! Maybe that other man is your *tata*." She directed his gaze toward the taller Marcel, who was standing nearby. "What about him?"

"No, no." Daniel shook his head stubbornly. "The little one is Tata!" He was the first one through the door when it opened, a tiny boy running straight toward the open arms of the short man and the sweet-looking lady who were waiting for him.

There were nine people altogether who had brought Daniel to the airport to meet his family—Lili's parents, three of her younger brothers, and three sisters. Before they left, they embraced Daniel and gave him a banana, and then asked to take a photo with him. Monica's heart ached when she saw the fear in her son's eyes, and he held on tight as she tried to put him down. She could almost see the wheels turning in his little mind. What was happening? Would he have to go back with Lili?

Hugging him close, she whispered in his ear, "Don't worry, Danny dear. You'll stay with us." But it was still hard for Daniel to understand the situation.

She watched her son intently as he joined Lili's family once more for the photo. How he had grown in the past six months! She had left a babyish toddler, and now he was a little-man toddler. How much had they missed out on in his life? It was clear that he did not hold a grudge against his parents for leaving him behind when they had escaped; he had come running straight to them when the door opened. But after six months of separation, they would be learning to know each other all over again.

How good it was to hear two pairs of little feet running through the house when they arrived home! How good it was to hear the giggles of two little boys as they played together, reveling in the bond they shared as brothers! Now Monica had two shadows as she moved about the small kitchen, cooking a special supper to celebrate Daniel's homecoming. Everything was new to him, and at times his remarks made her smile.

"It's a *little* bathroom!" he exclaimed when he entered it for the first time. "At my house, I have such a big bathroom." He waved his hands in a wide arc, trying to describe the spacious quarters to which he had been accustomed. Monica had to laugh, at the same time wondering how much the small boy would continue to remember as time went on.

"I want to read tonight from Romans 8:28," Nicu said that evening as they sat together in the living room. Benjamin and Daniel snuggled against him on either side of the sofa. As she looked at them, Monica thought her husband and sons made a picture that no camera could justify.

"'And we know that all things work together for good . . .'" Nicu glanced at her over Daniel's head, and Monica saw tears glistening in her husband's eyes. "God deserves all our praise for the miracles He has performed in our lives. What would we do without Him?"

Monica couldn't speak. Marcel and Christian were also silent. Monica's thoughts traveled back over the past six months—back to when they had first escaped from Romania and left their son behind, to this glorious day in February when he had returned. God had truly performed miracles in their lives. Nicu was right. They couldn't make it without Him.

20

Go or Stay?

Stepping back, Nicu surveyed the painted lids for electric heaters that he had hung up to dry. There were more waiting, but he wanted to make sure he had done the job right. Satisfied, he turned back and picked up another lid. He thought back to when he had started this job. It had been easier for Marcel to find a job since he knew German, but Nicu had taken a dictionary along when he had his job interview.

In the year since they had come to Nuremberg, many things had changed. The boys were enrolled in kindergarten, and they were all beginning to learn German. Day by day, Nicu and Monica's question was growing—would they stay here or go to America?

That night during the evening meal, Nicu listened quietly as Benjamin and Daniel chattered about their day at school. He couldn't help noticing the meager fare that Monica had prepared for their meal. Although they no longer had the threat of arrest hanging over their heads, they still had the stress of barely earning enough to make a living. Fortunately though, Marcel and his son weren't with them anymore. Sanda had joined her husband and son in Germany, and the family had moved into a house of their own.

While Monica washed the supper dishes and the boys played on the floor, Nicu sat at his desk, working out the figures. "We're barely making it," he announced when Monica came up behind him. "We hardly have enough money for food and clothes, not to mention all the utilities. Then there's the rent to pay—" He broke off.

"And we still have no answers from the German and American embassies," she said quietly.

"No." Glancing up, he met her gaze. "*Schatz*,[7] whatever will happen to us? Where will we end up?" He sighed and leaned back in his chair. "I really want to go to America, but I'm starting to wonder if it'll ever happen."

Monica leaned against the desk, her eyes thoughtful. "Perhaps we should start praying and ask God to give us our answer. He might have something different in mind for us."

"Are you saying you don't care if we don't go to America?"

Monica hesitated. "I really don't know, dear," she said softly. "All I can say is that wherever we go, my place is with you and the boys."

He was silent for a long moment, drumming his fingers on the desk. "Okay," he said at length. "Let's leave this up to God and take the approval that comes first as His will. If the approval comes from Germany to stay here, we'll stay. If it comes to go to America, we'll go there."

"In other words, we're putting out a fleece?"

"Yes, and trusting God for our answer."

"Monica, what are we going to do?" Nicu stood staring from one official document to the other on the table before them. "We received approval to stay in Germany and go to America two days apart!"

"We prayed that we'll do whatever comes first," Monica reminded him.

"So two days sealed our destiny? We're staying here in Germany?" Nicu ran both hands through his thick brown hair. "We have friends in America who would've helped us start out. It would have been good. Why does God

---

[7] German word for "treasure."

want us stay here when we wanted so much to go to America?"

Monica could only shake her head. She had no answers.

"Well, I think it's clear what we're supposed to do," Nicu said at length, taking a deep breath. "We prayed and told God that we would take whatever answer came first as His will. Our debts to the Romanians are already paid, and once I'm finished paying our debts to the Germans for getting us here from Yugoslavia, we should be able to get on our feet." He didn't add what Monica already knew—that he was also giving money to Romanian families in Germany who still had loved ones back home.

Nicu continued in a musing tone, "Now we finally know that we're staying here. But why?" He glanced through the window, gazing into the starry sky as if searching for an answer. But the heavens were silent.

Now that they had been granted political asylum to stay in Germany, their families from home could visit if they were able to obtain passports. Ana Bejenaru was the first to come, meeting Nicu and Monica at the airport with tears of joy. "Monica! Nicu!" She embraced her daughter and son-in-law. "It's so good to see you again!"

"And you, Mama." Monica wept on her mother's shoulder while Nicu stood looking on, tears in his own eyes. It was wonderful to see someone from home again. The boys were still at school, but he knew they would also be eager to see their grandmother.

They enjoyed every moment of the weekend, making the most of their short time together. "You have a nice place here," Ana commented when she entered the tiny apartment. "It's small but cozy."

"It hasn't been easy, but we're thankful for what we have," Nicu said, sitting down across from her at the table. Monica bustled around the kitchen, preparing coffee and ice cream to serve for a snack. "For a while I wasn't sure how we were going to make it. Monica did some cleaning jobs to help us survive."

"It sounds a lot like what's been happening in Romania," Ana said. "People hardly have anything to eat there, either. Ever since you left, things have been getting worse and worse."

Monica handed her a cup of coffee. "You must take some food back with you when you leave, Mama."

Nicu nodded. "Whatever little we have, we want to help," he declared.

But he didn't stop there. After Monica's mother left, Nicu arranged a meeting with a group of friends who had escaped to Germany from Romania. "The economy in Romania is steadily getting worse, and provisions for our brothers have been getting harder to find since we left," he told them. "These reports from home are sobering to me. I have gathered us together to pray for the situation."

Outside, the wind was rising and rain poured down on the roof. The atmosphere in the room was sober. Each one in the group also knew of the pressures their brethren in Romania were facing. One by one they prayed aloud, asking God to help the believers who were still behind the curtain of communism.

Nicu prayed last, asking for the Lord's direction as he conducted their meeting further. "I want to help our brethren by sending food parcels into Romania," he announced, looking out across the crowd. "We'll also be able to send parcels home with the friends who come to visit us here in Germany. Are we willing to come to their aid with the little we have? I'm trusting the Lord to provide."

Unanimous support was given for his suggestion, and Nicu closed the meeting with another prayer, placing their ideas into God's hands.

From this gathering of friends came a desire to meet regularly for worship. They decided to form a Romanian church in Germany, and Nicu consented to serve as their leader.

When Nicu's mother came to visit several months later, Nicu and Monica sent some food parcels back with her. "We really appreciate this, son. You're doing good things here," Catarina said, smiling. "The church you started has helped so much in providing what we need to survive."

"We still don't fully understand why God wanted us to stay here," Nicu responded. "But we can see at least part of His purpose in how we've been able to help our loved ones at home." He paused and then asked quietly, "Is Tata ever going to come visit us?"

"He wants to," Mama said, "but it might be quite some time. It takes money to travel, you know."

Nicu knew that all too well. After leaving Romania without saying goodbye, he was overjoyed that his mother could visit them. If only Tata were here too! How long would it be before they saw each other again?

"Here, Benny, let me help you with your coat." Nicu zipped up Benjamin's coat and turned to Monica, who was tucking a scarf around Daniel's head. "It's going to be cold out there tonight."

"At least we know how to dress for it." Monica's deep purple dress brought out the silky gloss of her brown hair, and her eyes sparkled. "It was always cold when we went Christmas caroling in Romania."

"Do you think the people here will like it, Tata?" Benjamin bounced from one foot to the other, his face glowing.

"I'm sure they will, son." Nicu grinned and tweaked his nose. "They might even give you some candy! When I was a little boy, the people used to give us nuts when we went caroling."

Together they left the house and went out into the snowy street, heading toward the church. Even though it was different to be in Germany for Christmas, they were enjoying it. With the little money they had,

Nicu and Monica had bought a few small gifts for their boys. They celebrated the special holiday at church with their fellow believers, and now they planned to go out with other Romanians to sing Christmas carols for the Germans.

After dividing into small groups, the Romanians went out into the streets. Standing before the houses, they sang Romanian songs for the people at their windows. Nicu wondered at the surprise on many faces. Weren't they used to this here?

Some of the people came out on the porches to listen. When they were finished singing, Nicu stepped forward to greet an elderly couple on the porch nearest them. "This is a real surprise," the man said, leaning on his cane. "We've never experienced anything like this."

"Thank you so much," his wife added, clasping Monica's hand. "We're happy you came out to sing Christmas carols for us."

"We're glad to do it," Monica said with a smile.

As the ladies visited, the man turned to Nicu. "Where are you from?"

"Originally from Romania," he answered. "We went Christmas caroling every year over there."

"Romania?" His eyebrows furrowed. "That's a communist country."

Nicu nodded. "Yes, but many people of faith live there."

"And what do you think of it here?"

Nicu paused before answering. Then he said honestly, "In Germany, you have religious freedom and money—everything you need. In Romania, we had to depend on God. Here, I've seen that people tend to forget how much they need God." He met the elderly man's gaze. "Why don't Germans have the strong faith they used to have?"

Silence met this candid question, broken by the sound of the frigid wind howling around them. By then Monica and the elderly man's wife were listening to their conversation. The man's silvery head bent a little, and there was sadness in his words when he answered, "It is as you say. When people have freedom and everything goes well, they tend to forget

God." Reaching out, he gripped Nicu's hand. "Keep up your faith, young man. We need more men like you who are willing to stand for the truth."

"God bless you," Nicu said, returning the warm clasp. After shaking the elderly lady's hand, he turned to join Monica and the boys. "Have a blessed Christmas!" he called over his shoulder.

"And the same to you!" They stood waving as Nicu's little family slipped back into the street to join their friends.

21

A New Mission

Rolling fields of wheat and corn stretched out under a vast blue sky, sweeping by in a blur as Nicu drove the family car down the highway. "I'm really looking forward to the conference this weekend," he said, glancing at Monica. "Ieremia Hodoroaba had a good idea in sending out invitations to other Romanian churches." Ieremia was a missionary pastor in France whom Nicu had learned to know through his church work.

She smiled. "I'm looking forward to it too. There's a program of preaching and singing, right?"

Nicu nodded. "Its purpose is so we can unite and fellowship and help each other."

"I wish it would be closer," Monica remarked. "Are there a lot of Romanians in Paris?"

"Not many." Nicu's brow furrowed. "Maybe we should organize a conference in Germany. Churches from all over Europe are coming for this, and Germany is more central than France."

He shared the idea with Ieremia a couple months later when the pastor visited Nicu's church. "It sounds good to me," Pastor Ieremia agreed. "I'm sure our brethren in Austria and Italy will be glad to come to a place that's more central."

"How is it going with your work of sending Bibles by mail into Romania?"

Nicu asked. Together they sauntered toward the church doors, stepping out into the balmy evening air.

The pastor smiled. "It's going well." Nicu knew that though he sent the Bibles by donations from other churches, Ieremia supported the work with his family's own money and personally did the work to send them.

"I have a burden on my heart to help pastors in Romania," Nicu shared quietly. "Recently I found out about a Christian mission that sends Bibles to communist countries. They have various ways to get the literature there. I plan to go to them and ask if they'll let me take Bibles and literature to the border of Yugoslavia. From there I want to send them into Romania."

Reaching out, Ieremia gripped his hand. "May God bless you for your desire to serve Him, Nicu. He is able to use people in a mighty way when they are willing to work for His kingdom."

Nicu leaned his head against the car seat, closing his eyes. Early morning sunlight shone through the window, slanting across the mountains surrounding them. He and his friend Muller had started out for Yugoslavia before daylight, and he was tired from driving. Hopefully he would be able to get some rest now.

The mission had willingly accepted Nicu's request to take Bibles to Yugoslavia and send them across the border. Knowing the Serbian language had made it easy for him to contact Yugoslavian churches and ask for brothers close to the border to smuggle the literature across.

"I'll be taking these trips three to four times a year," he explained to Monica. "I know it's difficult to support this work without much money, but I'm so excited to be able to help our brothers in Romania in some small way."

She studied his face and smiled a little. "You've always been burning for the work of the Lord, Nicu. It's one of the first things I noticed about you."

A NEW MISSION

It was a blessing to know that Monica shared his desire to help the believers of their native country. And from the beginning, Nicu loved his work. For each trip, he bought ten Bibles and took them to Yugoslavia, traveling with his friend Muller. The two men divided the cost of the trip and helped each other drive. Nicu also paid the Yugoslavian brothers who smuggled the literature. The men had passports that allowed them to cross the border into Romania for one day, so they took bags of Bibles along. Most of their families were poor, and Nicu offered them food that he had bought himself.

Nicu's dreamy state was startled to alert wakefulness when the car gave a sudden lurch. Beside him, Muller's face was white as he fought to keep control of the car while navigating around a sharp curve with no guard rails. The car bounced along the edge of the road before stopping. Looking down, Nicu gasped as he saw a deep ravine dropping away from the road. The right tire balanced on the edge of the ravine.

For a moment, silence sounded loud in the vehicle. Then Nicu took a deep breath, his voice trembling as he spoke. "I can drive now, Muller."

Without a word, his friend slid out of the driver's seat. They both knew that God's hand had stopped the car from going down over the deep ravine to certain death.

From where she stood stirring the cornmeal, Monica could watch the bustling street below. All along the street, hanging baskets of flowers adorned the windows. The bright, beautiful colors made her smile.

It was evening now, nearing suppertime. Sliding the finished cornmeal toward the back of the stove, Monica prepared to fry eggs. But her hands moved slower than usual, and more than once she stopped to stare out the window. Ever since Nicu had told her the story of how he and Muller had almost lost their lives, her thoughts had been full of turmoil. What if

Nicu left on one of his trips and never came back?

But that wasn't all. While she felt thankful that her husband was no longer under pressure from the government in his church work, lately a different pressure had descended over their family. As the pastor of their church, Nicu had begun helping Pastor Ieremia Hodoaraba organize conferences with churches all over Europe. With all the other responsibilities his position required, he was spending more and more time away from home.

"Lord, what can I do?" Monica asked aloud. "I wish Nicu would be home more and spend time with me and the boys. He's gone so much with his church work that even the boys have started asking—" She stopped short as the entrance door banged open. The boys were coming in from playing outdoors.

Benjamin dashed into the kitchen first, skidding to a stop beside her. "Smells good in here."

"Did you have fun playing ball?" she asked with a smile.

His eyes sparkled back at her. "Sure did! We almost won—"

A whoop broke into his words as a smaller version of Benjamin whirled around the corner. "Mama!" Daniel's cheeks were flushed, and his brown hair flew in all directions. "I forgot to tell you that we're having show-and-tell tomorrow at school. What shall I take?"

The next few minutes flew by as Monica exchanged lively chatter with the boys. But after they left the kitchen, her melancholy returned.

As she fried the eggs, Monica watched the boys playing together on the floor in the living room. Nicu would be home soon, and she could predict how their evening was going to be. After a quick supper, he would excuse himself early to attend a meeting at church, leaving her at home alone once more with the boys. Sometimes she felt as though they barely had any family time anymore.

She turned to the sink, grabbing a dishcloth. All at once everything seemed to grate on her nerves—the table that still needed to be cleaned and set for supper, the cluttered countertops, the dishes piling up on the sink. *Lord, what can I do?* The cry of her heart winged its way heavenward once again as she set to work. *It's been like this for months! Nothing is changing; in fact, it's getting worse. Please, won't you change Nicu and move him to spend more time with me and the boys?*

As she wiped the table, Monica seemed to see again the beaming bride in the mirror on the morning of her wedding day. For as long as she had known Nicu, he had prioritized his relationship with God. In the month she had taken to pray and fast for God's will, He had shown her clearly that Nicu was the one for her. She had had no qualms about their life together on the day of the wedding. With joy she had promised to follow her new husband and be his helper.

Was she staying true to her vows? Monica finished wiping the table and draped the dishcloth over the sink. Leaning forward, she looked out the window. The twilight sky was hazed with clouds, hinting rain. *The Lord gave Nicu to me, and I promised to help him in everything.* The thought struck her with sudden force, opening her heart to the painful truth. She had not been praying right about this.

Monica's eyes misted as she bowed her head and whispered, "Dear God, I ask you here and now to change my heart and help me to accept my husband how he is. I promised to be his helpmeet, to support him and pray for him. Please help me to truly be his helper!"

Feeling better, Monica set the table and turned back to the stove to finish her meal. As soon as Nicu came home, they would be ready to eat. But the test came when the door closed behind her husband after supper and a stillness settled over the whole house. The evening ahead looked so long. What were she and the boys going to do?

"Mama?" Benjamin tugged on her hand as they stood at the window watching Nicu stride down the street, Bible in hand. "Why is Tata at church all the time and not with us?"

Monica's heart twisted, and for a moment her commitment to accept her husband's calling wavered. Then she took Benjamin's hand and spoke gently. "Tata is doing God's work, son, and we need to pray for him." She reached out a hand to Daniel. "Let's pray together right now, boys." Without waiting for an answer, she bowed her head. When they finished praying, her heart felt at peace once again. When Nicu came home hours later, she was able to meet him with a smile.

22

News from Home

Sometimes a phone call at the Romanian collective farm office could take up to six hours to go through. In April of 1985, Ieremia Craiovan placed a call and waited for more than an hour until he heard his brother's voice on the other end of the line. "Hello?"

"Nicu, Tata had a stroke. We found him unconscious in the garden and rushed him to the hospital." Ieremia stopped, fighting tears. There was no sound from his listener. "Tata is conscious now, but he can't eat or speak," he went on finally. "The four of us brothers came and gathered around his bedside. Tata pointed up one finger, signaling that one of his sons is missing."

A cold shadow suddenly seemed to cross the April sun, and Nicu shivered. "I'll try to come, Ieremia," he promised. They were still waiting to receive German citizenship and would not be able to leave the country until then. He had planned to take his family for a visit to Romania as soon as they could—but now everything had changed without warning. Surely it was possible to receive paperwork to go home and see his dear *tata!*

But a week later, the telegram came. "Tata passed away. The funeral is in three days."

The news turned every color that had been glowing with early springtime beauty into drab, dull shades. Nicu stumbled homeward with tears in his eyes and a deep, heavy pain in his heart. He hadn't seen his father in five years. Now Tata was gone, and he hadn't even been able to say goodbye.

The next day he went to the officials, asking permission to go to his father's funeral. The man leaned forward across the desk, his eyes piercing and stern. "You can go, but we can't guarantee that you'll come back. You don't have German citizenship and are not under our protection."

Nicu bowed his head, vaguely realizing the man was advising him against going to the funeral because he knew it wasn't a good idea. But this was too much. With effort, he straightened his shoulders. "I'm going," he managed to choke out.

The man behind the desk grew sterner still, his clipped words striking Nicu's heart. "You have five minutes to decide."

Nicu knew then that the man was right—with his wife and children still in Germany, it wasn't a good idea to leave without knowing if he would ever come back. He turned and left the office, walking out into the street. Dark clouds were billowing across the sky, and rain pelted the cobblestones at his feet. He felt that he was drowning in a sea of grief too deep for tears. His father was gone, never to return.

The graveyard was lit with pale sunlight, its breezes chilling Nicu as he entered it. He stood just inside the gate, watching people gather around a distant grave that had been freshly dug. A sense of dread filled his heart. He hadn't been able to attend his own father's funeral; why join this gathering? Yet he somehow felt drawn to it.

As he reached the grave, the people parted silently, letting him step to the front. When Nicu looked down at the hole in the ground, his breath caught in his throat. The man in the coffin, lying still and pale in death, was his father!

Nicu's eyes widened as his father's eyes opened and looked straight at him. Then he stood up in the coffin and smiled tenderly at his son. As Nicu's vision blurred, Tata lay down again.

His heart breaking, Nicu turned and shouted to the people, "Why are you burying him? He's alive, not dead!"

Then Nicu's eyes flew open and he sat up in bed, his heart pounding. Starlight shone through the drapes over the bedroom window, and Monica was still sleeping beside him. He shook his head, trying to clear it. Had the vivid experience actually been a dream?

Slipping out of bed, he stepped to the window. In the week following his father's funeral, he had suffered much pain and tears. Unable to work for several days, he had stayed at home, feeling as though something within him had died. He had loved his father, and now there was nothing left but memories. If only he could have gone to the funeral and been with the rest of his family! What must his dear mother and brothers be going through? How he longed to see them all again!

Heavy of heart, Nicu gazed into the star-studded sky. His dream, he realized, was like a farewell for him from his father. Back when he had escaped Romania, he hadn't been able to tell Tata that he was leaving and couldn't come back. They had never seen each other again. But now, in the vision of his father standing up in the coffin and smiling at him before he lay down again, Nicu recognized a sign of peaceful departure that assured him they would meet each other in heaven.

"It is clear to me that my father still lives," Nicu whispered. "There's coming a day when I'll see him again." Bowing his head, he wept. But this time the tears that fell were tears of healing that stilled his heart with peace.

23

The Decree

In 1987, the border of Romania closed to aid from other countries. "We aren't that poor," President Ceauşescu had declared. "We don't need help from the outside." His decree stopped all the food parcels flooding into Romania, plunging the already desperately poor country into chaos.

Christian Aid for Romania, an organization established by Amish and Mennonite people in America, was also affected by this decree. They had been sending food parcels to Romania since 1981. At the time of the border closing, some parcels were still at a warehouse in Pennsylvania, others were crossing the ocean, and still others were waiting at Rotterdam.

What could they do now? Everything was stopped, and they had to do something with the parcels. Christian Aid began searching for other countries that could use them. Their search resulted in a decision to help the countries of Haiti and Nicaragua. But David Troyer, the founder of Christian Aid, still had a burden on his heart to help Romania. Could they somehow send food parcels secretly?

He spoke with Elena Boghian, a Romanian lady who worked in the office. She had come to America in 1983 and had started helping send medicine parcels to Romanian doctors a year later. "Is it possible to send bulk food from other European countries to Romania? Perhaps someone in Europe could take it across the border for us."

"I can look for someone who is willing to do that," she answered readily.

"Try this phone number," he suggested. "It reaches a Romanian family living in Austria. The man's name is Peter, and he had experience in transporting food, clothes, and secret literature into Romania before the border closed."

After David left the room, Elena dialed Peter's number. "Would you be willing to take food to poor families in Romania?" she asked. "We'll provide addresses, pay for the food, and also pay you for taking it."

"I'm sorry," Peter said regretfully, "but I'm too busy to take this on right now."

"I understand," she said. "But do you know of someone who will be able to help us?"

He hesitated. "I'll give you a phone number," he said at length. "I don't know what will happen, but you can contact him. The man's name is Nicolae Craiovan."

"What can you tell me about him?"

Peter's answer came without hesitation. "He's a dedicated Christian and the pastor and founder of a Romanian church in Germany. Nicu also works with a pastor in organizing conferences with Romanian churches all over Europe. You can trust him."

With the number written on her hand, Elena placed the next call right away.

When Nicu hung up the phone, he had the dizzying feeling that everything was about to change.

I want to pray and see if I'm capable of doing this work. Nicu stared unseeingly into the distance, the words he had spoken in answer to Elena Boghian's request still ringing in his mind. Was God truly calling him to work for this mission in America?

"I'm not a German citizen yet," he told Monica that night. "And I'm not used to the mileage or to handling such big amounts of money." Picking up the bread platter, he met his wife's gaze. "But it looks like something I might want to get into. I'm already involved in this in a small way, you know."

Monica hesitated, concentrating on the cup she was filling with water. Finally she looked up. "It would mean a risk at the border."

He nodded. "And what they're asking me to do is something on a much bigger scale than what I have been doing. The lady who called me is Elena Boghian, and she grew up in Romania. She lives in America now and works for Christian Aid for Romania."

"What's for supper?" Daniel dashed into the room, with Benjamin close behind.

"I have bread, cheese, and meat." Monica smiled at him and gestured toward the kitchen. "The cheese still needs to be brought out."

"I'll get it," Daniel offered quickly.

"Thanks." Monica finished filling the water cups and took her place next to Nicu, standing behind the chair. When Daniel joined them again, Nicu led in prayer.

"What were you and Mama talking about, Tata?" Benjamin asked after they were seated. Reaching out, he took a slice of bread.

"An organization in America called Christian Aid for Romania sends boxes of food into Romania for the Christians," Nicu explained. "When the border closed, everything was stopped. Now they want to find another way to take food in and are asking if I'll take the job. I said that I want to pray about it first."

Benjamin's eyes shone. "You already help poor people, Tata. Think of how much more you could do!"

"I thought of that too. But I don't know yet how big this work would be." He glanced at Monica. "I still have questions about it. Elena mentioned that Christian Aid will provide a fax machine so I can communicate with my employers."

Daniel looked up. "What's a fax?"

Nicu shook his head and smiled a little. "That's what I asked. She said it's a machine they'll use to send copied papers to me, and I'll be able to send back reports. I don't know how it's all going to work."

"They must have gotten good information about you somewhere," Monica commented. "These people would be trusting you fully. It isn't easy to find a person who will be honest when working with big amounts of money."

Nicu leaned back in his chair. "But if the border is closed and doesn't accept Christian Aid's food parcels, is it possible for me to take food over the border?" He glanced across the table at the boys. "Both of you need to help us pray that God will reveal what He wants me to do."

There was silence for a moment, broken by the sound of the coffee pot hissing on the stove. As Monica jumped up from her chair, Daniel changed the subject. "Tata, can you help me tonight with my homework?"

Nicu smiled and reached out to tousle the ten-year-old's hair. "Of course I will, son."

But as he helped Daniel with the math problems, he kept thinking about the money and the goods he would be entrusted with if he accepted Christian Aid for Romania's request. He prayed without ceasing throughout the next few days, weighing his decision from every angle. Then he received the good news. After eight years of living in Germany, his family had finally been granted German citizenship.

"This gives us the full right to enter Romania," he said to Monica that night. "Perhaps I could open a bank account just for Christian Aid and buy food in Romania myself. There are Romanian shops where only foreign money is allowed to buy items."

Monica didn't answer immediately. Stepping to the dresser, she picked up her hairbrush. "There's more to this decision than just the food parcels, isn't there?"

His gaze met hers in the mirror. "I keep thinking about the Bibles and literature," he said quietly. "If I take them in a car with food parcels, they will be easier to hide. The need in Romania is so great that the guards won't look for anything else—they'll be so glad for the food. But if I do this, we can't tell anyone."

He paused, but she said nothing. Sitting down on the bed, he reached for his Bible. "There's part of a verse in Esther 4 that has caught my attention, Monica. 'Who knoweth whether thou art come to the kingdom for such a time as this?' " Glancing up, he met her gaze. "All my life, God has had a work for me. I truly feel that He is calling me now to deliver food parcels for Christian Aid and smuggle Bibles into Romania."

Monica's hands stilled. "Smuggling Bibles is dangerous work, Nicu."

"It's God's work from the beginning," he reminded her. "Such a work is a pure work of faith; it's based on trust in the God I'll be traveling with."

Silence fell between them for a long moment. Monica felt her hands trembling as she set her hairbrush aside. Nicu was already gone so much with church work. This would take him away even more. And smuggling Bibles would place him in great danger. She shuddered even to think of what it could cost him—what it could cost all of them.

But she had been praying too, and sensed that God was indeed calling her husband to this work. As Nicu had said, it was God's work from the beginning, and such a work was based on trust in the One who called him to it. Could she remain at home with the same trust and confidence while her husband traveled with God?

Clasping her hands together, she turned to face him. "On our wedding day I promised to be your helper, Nicu. I won't stand in your way now." She paused, and her voice was just above a whisper when she spoke again. "But I will need to pray continually in order to keep from worrying about you."

24

The Precious Books

Nicu stood at the trunk of the car, loading everything inside as the boys brought it out to him. Ever since they had received German citizenship, he had a burden on his heart to visit their families in Romania. Now they had planned a trip for Easter, and excitement was running high.

"Here's another gift, Tata." Benjamin bounded around the car, a small box in his hands. His eyes sparkled. "I can't wait to see my cousins!" The boys, ten and twelve years old, didn't even remember some of their relatives. But this did not dim their enthusiasm for the trip.

As Benjamin ran back inside, Nicu placed the gift into the trunk. Besides their luggage, the car was filled with gifts and food for their families. He stepped back, looking it over. After the boys' suitcases were loaded, there wouldn't be much space left for the last thing he wanted to put in. But he wasn't about to leave it behind. This opportunity was too good to pass up.

Nicu strode into the house. Monica was nowhere in sight when he entered their bedroom and took the bag of Bibles from the dresser drawer. He had bought ten Bibles for pastors in Romania, taking advantage of this trip to deliver the precious books personally.

Closing the drawer again, he left the room. He found Monica in the kitchen, packing some last-minute items into a box filled with groceries. "I have ten Bibles here, honey," he said. "I want to take them with us too."

She hesitated, and a shadow crossed her face. "I don't think it's wise to take them this time, Nicu. Why don't you see how things go at the border first? Here, this box is ready. You can take it out with you."

He took the box and stepped out the door, pondering. He knew Monica's fears were legitimate. The border patrol guards always did a thorough search of vehicles that passed through, and it was especially dangerous to enter with Bibles. But they were going to cross a small border close to the village where his mother lived. Maybe someone he knew would be crossing the border as well, and he could give the Bibles to them after their car was checked and before his was checked.

Nicu decided to take the Bibles.

The countryside rolled by smoothly. Vineyards spread out under the twilight sky, and they passed lighted villages with tile-roofed houses. Germany had beautiful landscapes, but Nicu could hardly wait to get into the scenic country of his homeland.

They drove through the night, arriving at the border early the next morning. As Nicu stopped the car, he scanned the vehicles ahead anxiously. Then his eyes lit up. *Praise the Lord! He heard my prayer!*

"Monica, I see Yushi in front of us," he said, opening the door. "He's a brother to my best friend Feri from school. I'm going to talk with him." Without waiting for an answer, Nicu slid out of the driver's seat and hurried up to the vehicle directly in front of them.

"Yushi!"

"Nicu!" They embraced each other warmly. "It's been a long time, hasn't it?"

"It sure has. How are you? How is Feri?"

They visited a few minutes longer before Nicu changed the subject. "Yushi, God put you in front of me," he said, smiling. "When you open your trunk, I'm going to put a bag in."

Yushi looked at him curiously. "What do you have?"

Nicu didn't hesitate. His friend wasn't a believer, but they knew each other well. "Ten Bibles," he said.

Yushi's eyes widened. "Nicu—anything, but not the Bible!"

The words struck like a blow. Nicu managed to say goodbye to his friend and walked slowly back to the car, his head bowed. What was he going to do now?

As he slid into the driver's seat, Monica took one look at his face and asked, "What happened?"

Nicu hesitated but knew he had no choice but to tell her. Gripping the steering wheel, he spoke without meeting her gaze. "I brought the Bibles along."

He heard her catch her breath. After a moment she asked, "Well, didn't I tell you not to?"

In the back seat, Daniel leaned forward. "What's happening, Tata?"

Nicu stifled a groan and turned toward his son. "I have Bibles, and I can't hide them now."

Daniel was silent for a moment. Then his face lit up. "Put the Bibles around me, Tata, and close them up with my jacket. I'll stay in the car and play with my new toy." He held up the electronic toy he had been playing with and grinned. "I'll sit here and they won't look at me."

Nicu studied the ten-year-old. Perhaps he was right. To the guards, Daniel would simply be a young boy playing with his toy.

It didn't take long to put the Bibles around Daniel and tie them in place with the jacket. When Nicu was finished, no sign of the precious books could be seen. Getting back into the driver's seat, he drove up farther to the border, easing to a stop as a guard came to his window.

"All of you get out and take everything out of your car." The guard spoke stiffly, with no hint of a smile in his face. "We have to search you."

Nicu, Monica, and Benjamin quickly obeyed. Opening the trunk, Nicu took out the suitcases, food, and gifts they had packed, placing everything on the pavement.

Another guard from the border control came toward them, greeting them with a nod. "Good morning."

"Good morning, sir," answered Nicu politely. But his eyes were glued to the guard as he strode on—straight toward the car where Daniel was sitting in the back seat, playing with his new toy.

Reaching out, the guard tapped on the window. As Daniel rolled it down, he leaned forward. "What's your name?"

"Daniel." The boy's voice was calm, as though border patrol guards asked him questions like this every day.

"Can you still speak Romanian?"

"I do at home with my parents and brother."

"And what are you doing there?" The guard leaned forward even farther.

"I play and make points." Daniel held out the electronic toy with a winsome smile. "Do you want to play with it?"

"Yeah, show me." As the two bent over the toy together, Nicu closed his eyes briefly in silent prayer. The man was only inches away from the hidden books.

"I can't figure this out," he heard the guard say.

Daniel grinned. "You do it like this—" With a quick flick of his finger, he punched a button. "There! I scored a point."

The guard smiled and touched his head. "Brave one, you should keep on speaking Romanian."

Stepping away from the window, he came back toward Nicu. "I'll go through your things now," he said. They stood watching silently as the guard rifled through the food, clothes, and gifts. At last he turned to them. "You're free to go into Romania."

With the guard's words, Nicu felt as though a burden rolled off his shoulders. It didn't take long to repack everything and drive across the border, entering the familiar terrain. At a safe place Nicu stopped the car and turned to his son. "Oh, Daniel, you did such a good job!" He could not go on as tears filled his eyes. He knew—they all knew—that things could have turned out much worse at the border.

Reaching for Monica's hand, Nicu bowed his head. "Thank you, Lord Jesus," he prayed, his voice husky with emotion. "This wasn't how I wanted things to happen, but it was how you wanted it. Your angel protected us, and your precious Word is safe. Nothing is too hard for you. Praise your name!"

"Take some more meat, Nicu. Or mashed potatoes." Catarina beamed as she passed the dishes to him the second time. It was wonderful to be gathered around the table with his family again. Nicu sorely missed his father's presence, and he could see how his mother had aged in the past years. But this Easter was a joyful celebration with all his brothers and their families.

He couldn't help noticing, however, how the conversation centered on the country's poverty. "I still can't figure out why President Ceaușescu is restricting outside aid," his brother Samuel said. "Some are saying he's going to kill the Romanians."

Nicu leaned forward. "A mission in America recently asked me to deliver food into Romania," he said. "They are asking me to buy from shops where only foreigners are allowed to buy, and will provide me with the money and addresses. Most of my work will be in the northeastern part."

"Then we won't see you much here in the south," Mama remarked.

He smiled at her. "Probably not. But I'll visit you sometimes, you can count on that."

"Bring your family along when you can." Mama's glance took in Monica and the boys. "We don't see you nearly often enough. Your boys are growing up so fast; they'll soon be men!"

Laughter sounded around the table at this, and Benjamin and Daniel grinned. But as he looked across the table at his sons, Nicu felt sadness touch his heart. From now on his work with Christian Aid for Romania would be taking him away from home every month. But in order to do the Lord's work, sacrifices would have to be made.

25

The First Trip

"Will you take this camper into Romania with Bibles and literature?" As he spoke, Peter closed the door of the large motor home. The vehicle was inconspicuous in appearance, and a casual observer would never guess the secret it carried.

However, a casual observer wasn't the main concern. At the borders of Romania there would be guards, and there was always the possibility that the Romanian police would discover the secret compartments. This work of smuggling was dangerous, and not for the faint of heart.

But Nicu did not hesitate. Meeting Peter's gaze, he smiled. "I'll do that."

"This camper was once taken into Russia with Bibles and literature," Peter said. "The authorities found it and took everything away, but then our mission bought the vehicle back from them." Opening the camper's door, he stepped inside. "In here we hide the Bibles and literature in secret compartments. We can take three hundred Bibles at a time."

Working quickly, he showed Nicu how to close up the secret compartments. At length he took them all apart again and stepped back. "Now you do it."

Nicu was impressed with the ingenuity of the hidden compartments. But it was complicated. Two hours, then another, crept by as he worked alone, practicing to close up the secret spaces so that nothing could be seen.

At last he was finished. Peter came back to check on his work, nodding with satisfaction. "You can use this vehicle, and we'll put it in your name so you can go into Romania. For every trip, you'll be taking three hundred Bibles."

Reaching out, Peter gripped his shoulder. "I'm glad you want to do this work, Nicu. Brave people are needed for it. Before you leave, I want to pray for you and ask God to give you courage and strength to fulfill this calling."

He prayed with simple words, yet with feeling. As Nicu listened, his spirit was stilled with a gentle peace. No matter what the future held, this divine call to smuggle Bibles and literature into Romania, along with providing food parcels, had been laid upon his shoulders. Sufficient grace would be given to fulfill it, and the rest was up to God.

"I will stop here and pray," Nicu said, turning in his seat to face his passengers. The Romanian border was six kilometers away, and they were about to reach it with a load of food parcels, three hundred Bibles, and Christian literature. Entering Romania with this cargo would place their lives in grave danger.

Without further comment, Nicu bowed his head. "Dear Lord," he began softly, "we come before you now to ask your protection as we go from here. I know that your angel is with us, and we'll make it safely across the border if it is your will. Go with us and keep us. I pray this in Jesus' name. Amen."

"Amen." The earnestness in Nicu's prayer was echoed in the voices of the two young boys who listened. When the youth at the mission had heard that Nicu Craiovan was taking the mission's vehicle into Romania, they had wanted to go along. David and Andrew had joined him for the first trip. They planned to buy food and help pay for the trip, but as they neared the border, their tension was growing.

Long lines of vehicles were waiting at the border, the guards searching each one thoroughly. Nicu knew it could take twenty-four hours before his own vehicle was searched. In his mind's eye he reviewed the secret compartments again. Along with the three hundred Bibles and Christian literature hidden in them, there were also addresses Elena Boghian had faxed of the places to which he needed to deliver the food parcels. She had explained that most of the recipients were large families. It would be dangerous for those addresses to be found—both for him and the families that received the food parcels. They could be fined.

They reached the border at twilight. By then, brooding clouds had settled over the sky, and raindrops sprinkled the windshield, touching Nicu's face as he rolled down the window for the border patrol guard.

"I need to see your passport." For a moment the guard studied the document Nicu handed to him. Then he looked up and asked, "What is your name?"

"It's in the passport, sir."

The guard made an impatient gesture. "I asked what your name is, not where it is," he growled.

Nicu tensed but kept his voice calm. "My name is Nicolae Craiovan."

"Who are these people with you?" The guard peered at the two young men who occupied the passengers' seats.

"They're friends of mine, sir."

"Do you have guns? Pornographic magazines? Christian literature?" The questions were fired in rapid succession.

Nicu gestured toward his personal Bible, lying on the dash. "Guns and pornography do not go together with the Bible, sir," he said quietly.

The guard stared from Nicu to the Bible, considering and then seeming to accept his words. As he strode away, Nicu drew a quick breath of relief. His idea to have the Bible lying on the dash where the guard could see it had accomplished what he had hoped it would. No one, not even a hardened guard, could argue that the sacred book did not belong with guns and pornographic magazines.

But they still were not free to go. Another guard was approaching now, his bearing stiff and formal. "Unload your car, please," he said crisply.

Nicu obeyed, first reaching for the gift bag he had prepared for the guards. It was common knowledge that a person couldn't get past the border patrol guards without giving them gifts, and he had filled the bag with sugar, chocolate, rice, oil, and other things for the guards to divide among themselves. He waited long enough to see the man's eyes light up before turning to help Andrew and David unload the car.

For two hours they waited while the guards searched. Lightning forked through the dark clouds, and thunder rumbled in the distance. Still they waited. The wind was picking up when the guard finally turned and spoke to them. "Put your things back, and you can go into Romania."

When at last Nicu started driving again, the stormy night did not dispel the light that filled his soul. As he stopped in a dark field to get the addresses from the secret compartments, Nicu looked up into the sky, his heart singing praise to God for bringing them safely across the border.

Romania's roads were even worse than the roads they had traveled in Austria and Hungary to get there. Nicu swerved to avoid a dip, only to feel the camper's wheels jolt over a deep rut as he entered the town of Deva. They lurched around a curve, coming upon a scene that made Nicu's hands tighten on the steering wheel.

"We're going to be stopped here," he said in a low tone.

The others saw at once what he meant. A police officer was waiting for them up ahead. Andrew froze in his seat, and David took a slow breath. This was the fourth day of their trip, and they were entering the town early in the morning. Nicu had stopped to sleep at two-hour intervals the night before, driving on through the long hours to deliver food parcels. Until now, they hadn't faced any problems.

They stood off to one side, waiting while the police officer searched the camper. Finding nothing suspicious, he sent them on again. With relief, Nicu eased the camper onto the road again. He entered a side road, following the address that led to a church pastor's house. There he would deliver the food parcels for the pastor to divide among families. He knew that most of his addresses led to church pastors' houses. There wasn't much in the parcels—simple basics of sugar, rice, canned meat, and beans—but the joy he had seen in the faces of those who had received them was reward enough.

"There's an ordinary-looking car parked next to the road ahead of us." David's voice broke into his thoughts.

"It has three numbers on the license plate instead of four." Andrew had seen it too.

Tension knotted Nicu's stomach. Three numbers on the license plate meant the car belonged to the secret police. He forced himself to keep at an even speed as he drove past. A glance into the rearview mirror revealed that his wariness wasn't in vain. The car was pulling out onto the road behind them.

"Will I be able to shake them off?" he asked aloud.

Neither of the boys answered, and Nicu knew they were praying. Breathing a quick prayer himself, he turned left onto a side street. The car followed.

He drove down a hill and took another road that forked to the right. Once again their shadow followed, staying a little distance behind them. The driver was obviously trying to appear as if he wasn't following, but Nicu could watch every move the car made. Whenever he turned left, so did the car. When he turned right, it turned right.

Then his breath came faster. There was not only one police car now, but two that were following him. "It's time to get out of here!" he exclaimed. "I can't deliver anything as long as they're behind me."

"They must have orders from the officials in this town to watch all foreign cars." David sounded as nervous as Nicu felt.

"The problem isn't only for me if I stop to give food parcels," Nicu said. "The people I give them to would also be in danger. I think the best thing to do is simply leave and head on to Austria. This was going to be our last stop anyway."

"Will they search us again when we leave?" Andrew twisted to look back as they entered the main street. It was crowded, but he could still glimpse the cars following them from a distance behind.

"I think this officer will answer your question." Nicu was already stepping on the brake, having seen a policeman ahead flagging him down. As he rolled down the window, the officer strode forward.

"You are from Germany?" His eyes, narrow and penetrating, traveled around the interior of the vehicle before swinging back to Nicu. "Show me your passport."

Nicu handed it over, a flash of fear sweeping through him. What did this officer want? Would he always have a problem with the secret police following him when he entered this town?

To his relief, it didn't take long for the officer to search the vehicle and send them on. They reached the border of Romania by noon—a different location from where they had entered. Once again they had to answer questions and wait while the guards searched the vehicle.

When at last they were free to go, Nicu stopped at the first available gas station in Austria to call his wife. "I made it back safely, *schatz,*" were his first words.

"Oh, Nicu!" Her voice was edged with tears. "I'm so thankful. These past four days have been some of the longest days of my life."

And it's only the beginning. The unspoken words hung between them, heavy and tangible. Nicu brushed a hand across his eyes and spoke again. "I can't talk long, Monica, but I should be home this evening sometime." Though he knew it was expensive to call, he was reluctant to end their conversation. No doubt about it, the months ahead would be difficult for both him and his dear wife as his work separated them time and time again. But he was thankful that she supported him in it.

26

"God Is a Big God"

Monica had heard Nicu preach many times before, but this sermon struck her heart. He stood behind the pulpit, a light in his brown eyes as he looked up from his Bible. "God creates us with a plan in mind and prepares us for that work. Not only that, but He also protects and delivers us in our hour of need. How big is the God of those who trust in Him!"

Monica watched her husband intently. She remembered his words from several days earlier: "I can feel God in each step of this mission work of transporting food parcels for Christian Aid and smuggling Bibles into Romania. I started out with ten Bibles, and now I take three hundred. I couldn't do this if they hadn't asked me to work for them. I'm able to take food for the soul *and* the body."

Whenever Nicu left for a trip to Romania—which was twice a month, for three to four days each time—she had no way of knowing what was happening to him. To be sure, he called her as soon as he was able to let her know he was safe, but she was always acutely aware that each trip could be his last.

I could become a widow at any time! Monica shuddered, and her gaze found Benjamin and Daniel sitting with the other young boys at the front of the church. *And they could be left without a father!* How many times would she need to be reminded of her own father's words? *God makes no mistakes. Give your fears to God.*

She turned her attention back to Nicu. He was closing his Bible now and would soon be asking the congregation to stand for prayer. "God is worthy of our trust," he said, looking out over the crowd. "In Him we find peace and strength to do what He asks of us."

Monica studied her husband's face. There was a strength and confidence in it that told her he believed what he was preaching. No matter what it cost, he was willing to give his all for Christ's sake.

That knowledge stayed with her as Nicu dismissed the service. It resounded in her heart as she visited with her friends. That afternoon after the lunch dishes were washed, Monica took her Bible and went to sit outside on the porch. For a moment she held the sacred book close to her heart, gazing up into the sapphire sky. The book held the message for which her husband was risking his life. What did it mean to her?

Her head was bowed when Nicu stepped through the door behind her. "Monica? I saw you come out here." He paused, his glance falling on the Bible. "Maybe you want to be alone."

She shook her head and smiled faintly. "It's all right. I was praying and rededicating you to God." She met his gaze. "I know He prepared you for the work you do in Romania—you're strong and courageous. Even if . . ." She hesitated, and her gaze fell. For a moment she could not go on.

"No matter what happens," she said at last, "I've promised God that I will entrust your life into His hands."

Nicu was silent, looking out toward the street. It was quiet at this hour. A gentle breeze stirred through autumnal trees as two storks flew past them, landing on the roof of a towering building at the street corner. His sober expression made Monica wonder what he was thinking.

At last he turned to her and spoke quietly. "This morning in my sermon I said that God is a big God to those who trust in Him. On my travels to Romania, I'm discovering this more and more." He wrapped his arm around her shoulders, his sober expression brightening into a smile.

"Monica, I often feel the prayers that you and the boys send heavenward for my protection. My work is a great risk, but I know the Lord's angel is always with me."

The autumn air was crisp and chilly, with clouds layered in a gray-blue mantle across the sky. "It'll be around 11:00 p.m. before we reach the checkpoint of Romania," Nicu remarked, glancing at the clock.

"The town we're going to is really bad for driving, isn't it?" One of the three boys who rode with him leaned forward.

"I'm afraid so. The roads have a lot of holes and deep ruts."

Nicu fell silent then, listening to the others converse. As usual, the camper was filled with two thousand pounds of food, three hundred Bibles, and Christian literature. Since he knew how to answer questions at the border, Nicu always took the responsibility of driving across it.

The pale light faded slowly into darkness. The clock's numbers were showing 11:00 by the time Nicu drove into town. The camper's headlights pierced through the night, revealing an extremely rough street ahead. Nicu slowed down, but that didn't help much. As the vehicle bounced over a hole, he gripped the steering wheel with both hands, trying to steer around the next one. But he misjudged its width. They rocked into the deep chasm and stopped with a spinning of tires that raised dust and loose gravel.

"Why isn't this thing moving?" Nicu stepped on the gas, and the tires spun again. It was no use. Opening the door, he got out.

"One of the tires is flat," he announced minutes later, leaning through the door. "Will someone help me get this camper out of the hole so we can drive to a level spot to change the tire?"

The three boys wasted no time in joining him. But no matter how hard they strained to move it, the camper refused to budge. The literature and food had made it heavy and cumbersome. Finally Nicu stepped back, glancing at his watch. They had been working for thirty-five minutes with no success. He had taken off his coat long ago.

"Let me get into the driver's seat again," he said. "You boys push from behind while I push the pedal. Maybe this time it'll work."

They had already tried that numerous times to no avail. But he wasn't ready to give up yet. Getting back into the driver's seat, Nicu shifted gears and punched the pedal. The vehicle rocked forward but then settled back into place again. His lips formed a silent prayer as he pushed the pedal again. *Lord, what should we do?*

"It's not working," Nicu said finally, joining the boys. "Let's all work together to push the camper out again."

As they took their places, the sound of an approaching vehicle caught Nicu's attention. A small car came into view, deftly avoiding most of the ruts. The driver stopped when he saw them and opened his door, watching in silence as they strained once more to push the vehicle from the hole. Only when they had stepped back did he speak.

"Can I help you?" It was almost surprising that the gentle voice belonged to such a big man. As he unfolded himself from the car, Nicu turned to him, wiping the sweat from his brow.

"We can't do anything," he said simply.

"Maybe we can do it together," the man said, opening his trunk. "I have something here that should lift the vehicle from the hole enough to get the other tires on the ground." He maneuvered the jack in place, and once again they all took positions to help. This time the camper moved forward to level ground.

After the man helped Nicu change the tire, Nicu asked him, "Do you have a family?"

Closing his trunk, the big man turned to him. "I have eleven children."

Eleven? Nicu noticed a certain light in the man's eyes. He spoke again, quieter this time. "Are you a Christian?"

He smiled. "Yes, sir. I am a Christian."

"Wait here," Nicu said. Opening the camper door, he went inside and worked quickly to put a package of food together. "Take this home to your family," he said, smiling. "May God bless you."

"God bless *you*, sir!" With a flashing smile and wave, he was gone. Nicu stood still, watching until the car's taillights had vanished into the darkness. No other vehicles had come by at this time of the night. Why had this one?

As they drove on, Nicu was quiet, pondering what had just happened. *How big is the God of those who trust in Him,* he had said in his sermon on Sunday. Tonight—or this morning, since it was past midnight now—he knew beyond the shadow of a doubt that it was true.

They reached the town of Sibiu a couple hours later, where Nicu stopped in a dark field to open the secret compartments. He had to deliver literature in this area. Addresses in hand, he climbed back into the driver's seat and drove on.

It was an hour before daylight when they left town and headed into the mountains toward Suceava. Now that the literature was gone, Nicu could feel the difference. Not only was the vehicle lighter, but his tension had also subsided somewhat. From here on the trip would be less dangerous.

It's four hundred kilometers through these mountains, he mused. By now his passengers were sleeping, leaving him alone with his thoughts. As they had so often before, his thoughts turned toward home. *How are Monica and my sons making it through these long days? How blessed I am to have their prayers follow me wherever I go.*

It was also a blessing to have an understanding employer who didn't question him when he said he was going to take food into Romania. More than once Nicu had gone to his factory job directly from the interstate at 6:00 a.m. His boss always accepted that he was tired.

On and on he drove, the road winding ever upward through the mountains. The bad road made the distance seem three times as long. His drowsiness increased, but there was no time to sleep. Soon after daybreak he entered a small village where chaos reigned in the street, making driving difficult and dangerous. Wagons pulled by cows and horses were everywhere. Goats and sheep milled about the vehicle, and the cows refused to leave the street even when he honked the horn.

The din awakened his companions, and one of them got out to take pictures of the animals. When he joined Nicu and the othes again, Nicu carefully maneuvered the vehicle through a gate to a small house. By now the sun was coming up over the distant mountains, a great fireball that turned the eastern sky to gold.

It didn't take long to prepare a package for the family and take it inside. "Please thank the mission in America for us," the mother said with tears in her eyes. Children clustered around her skirts, peering shyly at Nicu and the young man who had come in with him. "We appreciate this so much."

"You have a nice family here," Nicu smiled. Reaching out, he tousled the dark hair of the small boy close to him. "Are you the oldest of your siblings?"

The boy grinned and nodded. They chatted a few minutes longer before Nicu turned to leave. Many other places still needed food parcels, but Nicu found himself humming as he slid back into the driver's seat. The day's work had just begun, and he'd had only two hours of sleep at intervals the night before. But it was all worth it when he saw that his work brought joy to these people's lives.

27

"God Led Us to This Place"

"What did you bring today, Craiovan?" The guard spoke less formally than usual as Nicu slid out of the driver's seat and squinted in the bright sunlight, trying to read the face opposite him. With all the trips he was taking across the border into Romania, he was beginning to recognize the guards—and they him.

"I brought a bag of food for you, sir," Nicu replied calmly. This guard was a psychologist, able to look into a person's eyes and read his soul. At the border it was important to be stoic and impassive, so as to appear calm and not offend the guards. The earnest prayers Nicu and his crew sent heavenward before they reached the border always helped. Even now Nicu could feel a quiet peace within, strengthening him for whatever lay ahead.

"Bring me a tape recorder next time," the guard was saying. "I need to see your passport."

"Yes, sir." Nicu handed it over.

The guard glanced at it briefly. "What's your name?" It was an unnecessary question, but protocol demanded it.

"Nicolae Craiovan," Nicu answered mechanically.

"Where are you going?"

"To Timișoara." By now he had learned to give the address of Monica's sister, who lived in Timișoara. He planned to leave from the border there after the trip was completed, rather than coming back to this one where the guards would be sure to ask why he had been in the country for such a short time.

"Who are these people with you?"

"Some friends."

The customs officer was approaching now. "Take everything from your vehicle," he ordered. Nicu quickly obeyed, waiting with the other young people while the guard searched their belongings. Two hours dragged by before they were finally released and allowed to continue on their way.

"We'll go to the town of Haṭeg first," Nicu told the others as they left the border behind. "I've never met Pastor Florin before, but we're supposed to go to his house." Checking both ways, he turned onto another road. "I called and told him we're coming," he went on. "Pastor Florin gave directions to his street and said to look for a house with an open gate. When we get there, we can just enter and close the gate."

For an hour he drove, passing barren fields in the onslaught of winter. Clouds hazed the pale blue sky, and a strong wind was whipping around the camper when he drove into town. The main streets were busy, with vehicles threading through throngs of pedestrians. Nicu slowed down, searching for the street number that would lead to the area where the pastor had directed him to find his house.

"The car we passed alongside the road a few minutes ago is following us," one of the boys said suddenly, glancing back.

"It has three numbers on the license plate instead of four," another added.

Nicu's hands tightened on the steering wheel as he glanced into the rearview mirror. A car was indeed following them, staying a little distance behind, yet close enough to keep them in sight.

Breathing a quick prayer, he turned onto the first side street he saw. Their shadow followed. He took another turn, and again the inconspicuous-looking car came after them. He whipped into yet another turn and noticed that it was Pastor Florin's street. Scanning the houses, he noticed one with an open gate. He sped up to it and entered quickly, jumping out to close the gate behind him.

When he turned, a man was standing at the doorway of the house. As Nicu strode forward, he came down the steps. "Hello," Nicu called politely. "Are you Pastor Florin?"

The man shook his head, looking puzzled. "No, sir. Why are you here?"

Nicu squared his shoulders. "The police were following us, and we had directions to enter where a gate is open," he explained. "We saw this gate open, so we entered. You aren't the pastor?"

"No. But don't be afraid," he added kindly. "I'm a Christian too. I know where Pastor Florin lives—his house is on this street. We'll wait a little to make sure it's safe, and then I can take you there."

"I appreciate this," Nicu said gratefully. He glanced toward the gate. The police car was nowhere in sight.

"God led us to this place," he told the youth when he slid back into the driver's seat. "The owner is going to take us to Pastor Florin's house."

The pastor was waiting for them when they arrived. Nicu backed the camper up to the house, and they spent the next minutes unloading the food and literature.

"I'll divide these goods among people who live in the north," Pastor Florin told Nicu. "I can't do it publicly in our church. There's always a possibility of having people in the church who are informers."

Nicu nodded without comment. He had needed information about Pastor Florin himself to be able to trust the man. As his trips became more and more frequent, he was learning to place his full confidence in the Lord in order to receive divine guidance and protection.

After the camper was empty, they left Romania, reaching Hungary by mid-afternoon. Nicu steered onto a rough street, slowing down to avoid potholes and ruts. "Look, boys," he said as they came up behind a truck. "They have hams hanging in there."

"It isn't good for me to see that," one of the boys groaned, rubbing his stomach. "It's been too long since lunchtime."

Nicu grinned and stepped on the pedal, driving up beside the Hungarian truck. Rolling down his window, he called out, "You can give us one too!"

The driver glanced over, looking startled. Then he smiled and pulled ahead. Once in front of them, he stopped and got out. "I'll gladly give you some ham. And I don't want any money," he added, holding up one hand as Nicu began opening his wallet. "Consider it a Christmas gift."

Nicu laughed and shook his hand. "Thank you, sir!"

"God gives us interesting surprises sometimes," Nicu remarked, still chuckling as he climbed back into the motor home. "This is a large ham—quite enough for everyone!"

They were all smiling as they offered a prayer of thanks and continued on their way.

"Tata!" Benjamin was the first to meet him at the door, with Daniel at his heels. "You made it back!"

Minutes later the four of them gathered around the table, holding hands while Nicu led in prayer. Giving thanks to God was always the first thing they did as a family whenever he arrived home from a trip.

Afterward, Monica served coffee and cookies while Nicu told them about his trip. "We went to the the town of Deva last," he said, taking a sip of coffee. "As soon as we entered, we were stopped and searched. When I drove away, I had this feeling that someone was following."

The boys listened, their eyes wide as Nicu went on. "I didn't know what to do. Should I go farther than I'd said I would? Then I saw them—two secret police cars following us. So we left without delivering anything." He shook his head. "I hardly ever do deliveries there, because they follow me all over."

Then his face brightened with a smile. "But let me tell you how I found

Pastor Florin." The kitchen grew completely silent as he described the scene—the moment he had spotted the police car behind him, the turns he had taken to avoid it, and the open gate he had entered and closed behind them. "God led us to that place," Nicu concluded. "We could have landed in a hornets' nest when we entered the gate. But the owner was a Christian, and he knew Pastor Florin. He took us to the pastor's place."

Monica sat still, amazed. She always prayed without ceasing while Nicu was gone, never knowing what was happening to him. The possibility that he might not come back someday hung over her like an oppressive shadow. Yet it was obvious from Nicu's stories that God's hand was on him. No matter what happened, He would use Nicu's work for His glory.

28

Divine Encounters

Pale light shrouded the city of Simeria as Nicu drove toward it. At 5:00 a.m. there were only faint stirrings of life in the streets. He shifted in his seat, forcing his heavy eyes to stay open. He had been driving all night from Germany to Romania. The other three passengers were sleeping, and the large motor home was silent. He longed to rest as well, but he knew he had to keep going and deliver all his goods.

Straightening, Nicu gazed ahead. The city's main street was only a few meters away now. Railroad ties ran across the road, with stones lying between the tracks. Scanning the mostly empty street, Nicu decided to cross the tracks and enter Simeria.

He was halfway across when he realized his mistake. The camper's wheels sank down into the stones between the ties and the axle caught on the track, bringing the vehicle to a dead stop. Try as he might, Nicu could not make it move, forward or backward.

Then it happened.

The first low rumbling sound made Nicu freeze. Within moments the long train was speeding around a distant corner, its whistle blasting. As the deep, mournful sound echoed around him, Nicu punched the pedal in one last desperate effort to move. Nothing.

The train's whistle sounded again. It would soon bear down upon him—and he could not move. So this was it. After all his hard labor to fulfill the calling God had laid on his shoulders, leaving his beloved wife and children at home month after month, it would end like this! His secret would be out, and dreadful consequences would follow.

Out of nowhere, a large German semi roared up behind him. Taking in the situation at a glance, the driver stopped the semi and jumped out. Hurrying toward the camper, he disappeared behind it. With utter amazement, Nicu heard clanking sounds coming from the backside of the motor home. Then, slowly, the hulking vehicle shuddered backward off the track as the train came into view.

Only seconds after the semi driver had pulled them to safety, the train rushed by. Nicu slid shakily from the motor home and stood with the others, watching it go. One of the boys took a picture of the train as it grew smaller and smaller in the distance.

Only after the train had vanished did Nicu turn to the semi driver. Gripping their rescuer's hand, he tried to speak. "You . . . you . . . came at just the right time, sir. I didn't think—" He stopped, unable to go on.

The men looked down at the chain that had pulled their van to safety. Strong wires woven together made it look like an iron rope. "It's amazing that you had this with you," one of the boys said quietly.

"Someone was looking out for you," the semi driver declared.

Nicu looked down the train tracks again and could do nothing but shake his head. As never before, he realized that he was under divine protection. There was work for him to do, and until that work was done, nothing could hinder it.

Nicu reached the town of Beiuș a couple hours later. The moon cast a pale glow over dark clouds as he backed the camper up to a pastor's house and opened the door. "We brought you some more food parcels, pastor."

"Unload it into my cellar," the pastor directed. They worked together until at last the cellar was filled. "I'd like to send this with the visitors who came yesterday," the pastor remarked, looking over the packages. "Do you know Elena Boghian?"

Nicu smiled and nodded. "She's my contact for the organization that sent this aid."

"Elena's sister Lidia is here right now," the pastor explained. "Recently I visited the States and met with Lidia's husband Gicu at a Romanian church. Gicu lives in Ohio now, and he sent a suitcase for his wife along home with me. Lidia and her brother-in-law Samuel traveled more than twelve hours to come here to pick it up." His brow furrowed thoughtfully. "The families in our area are poor, but the families where Samuel and Lidia come from are poorer. I think I will send plenty of this food back with them."

Nicu spoke quietly. "I feel certain that God has a special plan for my work. On the way here we were nearly hit by a train." He shared his story, stopping more than once as the memory, so fresh in his mind, choked him with emotion.

The pastor was quiet for a long moment after Nicu finished. The moon was brighter now, shimmering above them with a silvery radiance. Reaching out, the pastor placed a hand on Nicu's shoulder. " 'For He shall give His angels charge over thee, to keep thee in all thy ways,' " he quoted softly. " 'They shall bear thee up in their hands, lest thou dash thy foot against a stone.' You are indeed doing God's work, Nicu, and His hand is upon you."

"I think everything is ready, Tata."

"Thanks, boys," Nicu said, smiling. "You did a good job." Daniel and Benjamin had both helped him load the camper for the trip. They were always willing to lend a helping hand in this job, and Nicu knew they would pray for him while he was gone.

Germany had three holidays in May, and Nicu was taking an extra day of vacation on the first holiday for this trip to Romania. Drawing the money from his bank account with Christian Aid for Romania, Nicu had spent over three thousand German marks on food to take along. Three passengers would be riding with him.

"Let's go inside," Nicu said to the boys. The spring wind was gentle and balmy, carrying with it the sweet scent of flowers as they headed toward the house. Monica had hung a flower basket from their window, and the colors were a gleam of brightness in the twilight.

She was waiting for them at the door. "Is it time?"

"It's time, *schatz.*" He took her hand and looked into her hazel eyes, searching past the apprehension to the peace in their depths. It was always there, no matter what they faced. Not only had his faith in God grown stronger in the past months, but so had hers. When there was no one else to depend on, they found their Savior's grace sufficient.

Joining hands with the boys, they prayed together. They prayed for protection over Nicu, and also for Monica and the boys as they remained at home; for grace and strength to make it through the days ahead; for peace in knowing they were doing the Father's will, no matter what it cost.

Twilight had deepened into night when at last Nicu said goodbye to his family and opened the door.

"It's my midnight friend!" The pastor met Nicu at the door, smiling broadly.

Nicu grinned as they shook hands. "I always get here at midnight, don't I?"

"We'll unload everything in the usual place," the pastor said, leading the way inside. He stopped in a room at the end of the hall, small and ordinary-looking at first glance. But Nicu knew what was coming next.

Striding toward one wall, the pastor moved it back to reveal a hidden room behind it. The next minutes were busy as they unloaded all the Christian literature into the hidden room. When at last the pastor moved the wall back into place, there was nothing to indicate the secret behind it.

"Where are you going from here?" the pastor asked as they left the room.

"To the town of Bistrița," Nicu replied.

Reaching out, the pastor gripped his hand again. "May God bless you and keep you in your travels, my midnight friend."

Three cars were waiting in Bistrița to receive the load of food that Nicu brought. A pastor drove one car, Samuel drove another, and his sister-in-law Lidia rode in the third vehicle with her neighbor. Though the neighbor wasn't a believer, he was willing to help.

"We'll have to the take the back roads on our way to church," the pastor told the other two drivers. "There are a lot of police on the main roads."

They nodded solemnly. The night had grown cool, and there was a strong wind blowing. Clouds scuttled across the sky, blotting out the moon and stars. Together they set out—three cars loaded with food, driving single file through the darkness. Half an hour went by, bringing them to a railroad that crossed the main road.

Samuel went first, driving his car up the steep bank and crossing the railroad. As his lights disappeared around a sharp curve, the second car sped up the bank and over the railroad. But the driver took the sharp curve too quickly. The car's right tire dropped off the edge of the road, sinking toward the deep ditch below. There they balanced—slanting at a sharp angle, unable to go any farther.

Inside the car, Lidia felt the air leave her lungs as she looked downward. "Don't get out!" she cried to the driver. "I'll go into the ditch, and we'll be in terrible trouble!"

Behind them the pastor had stopped, and Samuel was turning around. Soon both men were struggling to pull the car back onto the road, but to no avail. By now the wind was whipping through their jackets with a penetrating chill. At this hour, there were hardly any other vehicles on the road. What were they going to do?

Many prayers ascended to the heavenly throne as the men continued straining to move the car. Inside the car, Lidia was praying too. But it looked hopeless. Filled with food, the vehicle was heavy and hard to move.

Out of the darkness appeared a man riding a bicycle. Seeing their predicament, he steered toward them and stopped. "I'll try to help you," he said, and the words were a welcome sound to the ears of the weary travelers. "But first, the ones inside the car need to get out."

The driver and Lidia obeyed quickly, crawling through the door closest to the road. Samuel, the pastor, the driver, and the bicyclist took their positions. Little by little, the car moved away from the ditch until at last it was on the road again.

"You're an answer to prayer," the pastor said, shaking hands with the stranger. "We didn't know what we were going to do."

The bicyclist's eyes lit up. "You are praying people, right? I'm a Christian too."

"Do you have a family?" Samuel asked.

"I certainly do." He grinned. "Many young ones who keep me hopping."

They laughed together, and the pastor said, "Wait here." The others kept visiting as he headed toward his car, returning minutes later with a food parcel. "May God bless you and your family," he said simply.

Straddling his bicycle, the man's smile seemed to light up the night. "God bless *you!*"

As he disappeared into the darkness, the others prayed together, thanking God for His protection. Lidia wondered what her unbelieving neighbor was thinking. Once again, God had been right on time, sending help in their hour of need.

Two hours later they reached their destination, where they unloaded the food into the pastor's church house. Lidia stood at a distance, watching the road until the precious cargo was concealed in safety. Dangerous as this work was, there was a blessing in knowing it was God's work and He was with them.

Priorities

Warm spring sunshine cast its rays over the people milling about the church parking lot. Monica stood with three of her friends, listening in silence as they chatted.

"We went to Switzerland for the holidays," Anna said. Short and red-haired, she was a vivacious lady who could always make Monica smile. "It was a wonderful time together, just relaxing with our family."

"Did you go to the Alps?" Elsa asked.

"Oh, yes. They are beautiful! We took a train ride up the Jungfrau, one of the highest mountains there. I would encourage anyone to go!"

"Last year our family went to the mountains for a family vacation," Sanda commented.

"We thought we might try something different this year," her husband Marcel said, joining them. He glanced at Monica. "Are you going anywhere for a family vacation this year?"

Monica hesitated. "We haven't talked about it."

"Nicu's gone again today, isn't he?" William remarked, coming up behind his wife Anna in time to hear the last of their conversation. Elsa's husband Robert was right behind him. "This is the second time he's been gone this month, right?"

She nodded, hoping they would start talking about something else. But

William was going on. "He certainly is dedicated to his work. Gone a lot through the week and also on weekends." He grinned teasingly. "I guess we'll have to start calling you 'the happy widow.' "

The others laughed, and Robert asked, "Why do you allow Nicu to be gone so much?"

Though she knew they were only teasing, Monica was in no mood to play along. She forced a smile, but her lips felt stiff. "I suppose you'll have to ask him," she managed. She turned to look for Benjamin and Daniel. It was time to go home.

Monica's thoughts churned in a whirlpool of confusion as she walked down the street with the boys. She knew that Nicu felt at peace about leaving over the weekends. By this time, his oldest brother Ilie had also moved to Germany and was working as a leader in the church alongside Nicu. He could trust that Ilie would do well. But would it be this way for the rest of their married life, with separations and the stressful uncertainty of not knowing for days at a time whether her husband was dead or alive?

She thought back to the time they had escaped Romania. Leaving their baby behind, Nicu imprisoned while she was placed in the retired policeman's home . . . even now she shuddered to remember those events. The eighteen days of separation had felt like an eternity. She had wondered then if God was preparing them for something, but she had never dreamed of this.

They had reached home by now, and there was no time to think about it anymore. The boys set the table while she prepared platters of meat and cheese and took fresh rolls from the oven.

"I hope Tata will call today," Benjamin said after prayer. He spread his roll with butter and reached for the cheese platter.

"Some of my friends were talking about how they went to Switzerland," Daniel announced abruptly. He pushed a lock of brown hair from his forehead, his face wistful. "Mama, I wish we could go to the mountains too."

Benjamin's eyes lit up. "I would love to go to the mountains!"

"So would I," was all Monica could say. Tears stung her eyes as she bit into her dinner roll. It had been a long time since the four of them had gone on a family vacation.

Nicu called that afternoon, saying he had made it safely back to Austria and was on his way home. As she hung up the phone, Monica made a decision. When Nicu arrived, she would tell him about the boys' desire to go to the mountains for a family vacation. There was one more holiday this month. Nicu had already taken trips to Romania over the other two; surely this one could be spent with his family.

The idea sparked an excitement within her that she hadn't felt for weeks. But she was hesitant to bring up the subject. She had an uneasy feeling that she already knew what his answer would be, and she didn't want to get her hopes too high.

That week they held midweek services, with an absence of several families. "Robert and Elsa's family went on a vacation," Monica said to Nicu that night. "The boys were hoping we could go to the mountains." Nicu was silent for a long moment after she finished speaking, his expression unreadable. Monica watched his face anxiously. Wasn't he going to say anything? Didn't he think the idea was a good one?

At last he met her gaze, and the look in his eyes told her what was coming. "I'm planning to take another trip to Romania on that holiday," he said slowly. "I meant to tell you, but . . ." He paused as though groping for words and then fell silent.

"Oh." The word sounded flat. She had thought she was ready for this, but evidently she had allowed her hopes to rise too high after all.

"You understand, don't you?" Nicu stepped closer.

Monica didn't trust herself to talk about the issue. Turning away, she pulled up the bed covers. "Of course," she said without emotion. "I'm going to sleep," she added quickly, hoping to evade any more questions that would certainly bring tears to the surface. He stood there for a moment and then turned silently away.

They did not discuss it again that night. But as the days passed and Monica still refused to talk about it, discouragement threatened to settle over Nicu. He hated the wall that was slowly building between them, but he felt helpless to break it down. God had called him to this work, and he couldn't go against that. Yet he also knew how difficult it was for his dear wife.

He spent extra time in prayer, pleading with God to protect their marriage from the enemy's attack and help Monica to accept their circumstances. Only He could make this right.

Monica sat on the bed, paging listlessly through her Bible. She hadn't been getting much out of her personal devotions these days. She knew her husband was doing the Lord's work, but her heart rebelled against the cost. They had to give up so much for it—family time, vacations, weekends. Her hands slowed, and she found herself staring down at the love chapter. When was the last time she had read it? Now the words seemed to leap off the page. "Charity suffereth long, and is kind . . . seeketh not her own . . . beareth all things, believeth all things, hopeth all things, endureth all things. Charity never faileth . . ."

Monica closed her eyes, too stricken to read any further. Her selfish desires were keeping her from accepting the call God had laid on her husband. How clear that was now! If she refused to accept Nicu's calling, how would it affect his ministry? *Oh, God, forgive me,* her heart cried. *I've been failing Nicu, and most of all, I've been failing you!*

There were tears in Monica's eyes when Nicu came into the room minutes later. He paused beside her, his glance going from the Bible to her face. "Are you okay?"

"I'm all right." A tremulous smile touched her lips. "God has been working in my heart, that's all."

He said nothing, but his gaze became intense. She took a deep breath. "Dear, I want to support you in your work, but it isn't easy. You're gone so much, and the boys are growing up. Benjamin is thirteen now, and Daniel is eleven. They need their *tata.*" She could feel her composure beginning to crumble again, but she kept on. "Last Sunday at church, some of the men were joking with me about being 'the happy widow.' They asked why I let you go away so much."

"What did you say?"

"I told them to ask you."

"They never said anything about it to me." He sighed a little. "Probably couldn't get up enough courage." He sat down on the bed beside her, still studying her face. "But you know why I'm doing this, don't you?"

This time she was ready with her answer. "I've never doubted that God called you to this, Nicu. I don't want to work against your calling." She glanced down at her Bible, and her voice softened. "When we got married, there were two promises I made to you—to be a loving wife, according to 1 Corinthians 13, and to be your helper. These are still my promises."

He was silent for a moment, tears glistening in his eyes. "I'd really like to take you and the boys along on some of my trips, *schatz,*" he said softly at length. "I truly feel like I'm living with God in this work. When we have a need, He's always there."

"Perhaps we could go with you this time." She saw the question in his eyes and smiled. "Truly, Nicu, it doesn't matter if we give up family vacations for the Lord's work, but I want to be more involved in the work. It's not just you in this—I'm here beside you. We're in it together."

The relief in Nicu's eyes was blessing enough. Long after he was sleeping, Monica lay awake, silently communing with God. It wasn't easy to see her husband leave month after month, but she had peace in knowing that their marriage was the Lord's perfect will. She wasn't "the happy widow" at all, but a blessed wife.

"I think we'll stop here." Nicu glanced in all directions before he pulled into the parking lot. It was empty—perfect for what he needed to do. "This is going to take a while," he said to Monica. "Several hours."

She nodded, noting the fatigue that lined his face. If only she could help him! But she knew that closing the secret compartments was a complicated task. As Nicu slid from the driver's seat, she turned back to her crocheting.

Moonlight shone through the window of the camper, and the boys were sleeping. This was the fourth day of their trip, and by now they had distributed all the food and Christian literature. After Nicu finished closing all the secret compartments, they would head homeward.

Settling deeper into her seat, Monica focused on her needlework. She was glad for this experience. It had helped her become more familiar with what her husband did every month; and when she saw the joy on the faces of those who received the goods, she understood why her husband loved this work.

An hour crept by as Nicu worked to close the secret compartments. At times vehicles passed by on the road, but no one stopped. Another half hour dragged by. Monica's fingers flew as she wove red, blue, and yellow yarn together, creating a soft blanket.

Without warning, a bump jolted through the camper, causing her needle to jerk to a halt. Monica gasped and straightened abruptly. It was not a mistake that the police car outside had run into the motor home—she was positive of that.

Behind her, Nicu was already springing into action. As he flung himself down on the bench and closed his eyes, she turned back to her crocheting with trembling hands.

Seconds later, the officer tapped on the window. Breathing a quick prayer, she opened it.

"What are you doing here?" The officer looked past her, searching the dark interior of the camper. The boys were still sleeping, and Nicu was lying motionless, his breathing deep and even.

"My husband is very tired, sir, and we stopped to rest a little bit." It was a wonder she could speak so calmly. Her heart was pounding so hard that she was afraid the officer would hear it.

His gaze swept the interior of the camper again, and Monica forgot to breathe. The secret compartments were still open in the back. Would the officer enter and search?

Time seemed to stand still in the moment it took for the officer to make up his mind. "Then good night, and happy resting!" Without waiting for an answer, he turned and strode back to his car.

Monica stared at the police car until its lights had vanished in the darkness. *Even if we trust God and pray, we never know what's going to happen in the next moment.* As the thought flashed through her mind, she shuddered. God had surely been near, giving her the courage to act calmly in spite of her fear.

But Nicu faced danger like this on every trip he took into Romania. Turning, she watched the dark figure of her husband as he finished closing the secret compartments in the back. His experiences proved over and over again how powerful God was in His ability to protect His servants.

Nicu sat at his desk, writing a list of what he had spent on the trip to Romania. Everything had to be reported to Christian Aid—what he had done with the items, where he had taken them, and how he had divided them up. Because of the danger, he couldn't write anything on the road, but he had a good memory.

"I want to draw more money from my bank account with Christian Aid for Romania next month," he said, glancing up. Monica stood in the doorway, watching him. "I was thinking maybe I'll spend 4,000 German marks' worth of food." He leaned back in his chair. "With what I spent in May, it will make 24,085 German marks altogether."

"It's a good thing we have a bank here in Germany that allows money from the American bank to go directly to it," she remarked.

He looked thoughtful. "God never fails to provide for our need, does He? It's the only bank we can use to do this."

Monica glanced at the map on the wall behind him. Nicu had highlighted the roads he traveled in Romania, and they extended all over the country. Giving up family vacations was trivial in comparison with the poverty that the Romanians were facing. Here in Germany the economy was all right, but the people of their native country scarcely had enough to live on.

What was going to happen to Romania? As long as President Ceaușescu restricted outside aid, they would plunge deeper and deeper into poverty. The situation was desperate.

But people were trying to help. They were involved in a good work—the Lord's work—and Monica was glad to work behind the scenes, supporting her husband and praying for him as he ministered to the Romanian people.

30

Not Alone

"You may be dismissed. Go in peace."

Bible in hand, Nicu stepped down from the pulpit as the congregation dispersed. It was a beautiful Sunday morning, crisp and bright in early autumn. Ethereal sunrays slanted through the sanctuary windows. He stopped to shake hands with a young woman nearby, lingering to ask her a question. "Would you know of someone who would be willing to assist with transportation when we go to Romania? We lack the third person for our next trip."

"I do know of someone," she said with a smile. "I would be willing to ride along." With sparkling eyes and an open, honest face, Renata was a girl of strong faith. Nicu had no problem accepting her offer.

Having never gone before, Renata saw the trip as a large and uncertain venture. With a trailer attached to the back of the motor home, they traveled many hours on the road, finally stopping a short distance before the border of Romania to do their customary praying.

Border guards with handguns holstered on their belts met them at the border, ordering Nicu to take everything from the vehicle. Renata and the boys helped him before standing back, waiting while the guards searched through the goods.

As she watched the bustling activity around them, Renata sensed something strange. They stood alone in the midst of men who were not friendly to their cause, knowing the secret compartments could be discovered anytime—yet the intense feeling that they were not alone grew within her as the minutes passed. *It's as though angels are standing around us,* she mused, awe filling her being.

Dark clouds were billowing across the sky when at last they received permission to cross the border into Romania. Within the next hour the skies opened to unleash torrents of rain, and the camper's headlights pierced no farther than a few feet ahead. Nicu slowed down, but the thick sheets of rain made it hard to see.

Without warning, an ominous *bang* reverberated in their ears, startling them all. "What's going on?" exclaimed Nicu. Steering to the side of the road, he opened the door and jumped out into the pouring rain. Minutes later he opened the door again. "The trailer is ruined—it broke down," he said hurriedly. "We must get help and try to find a part for it."

As the two young men joined him, Nicu glanced at Renata. "Are you okay with staying here by yourself?"

She nodded, but as the door closed behind them, her courage wavered. She was all alone on a stormy night with a motor home and trailer filled with food and Christian literature. *Would they return? What if someone—*

Renata shook off the thoughts. God was with her, and His angels surrounded her. Hadn't she felt them at the border? She was not alone.

It wasn't long before Nicu and the boys returned with what was needed to repair the trailer. They prayed together once again before they set out, thanking God for His continued blessing and protection.

It was still raining three hours later when Nicu stopped at the end of a long lane that led to a small house. "I can go in here by myself," he told the others. Stepping into the back, he quickly put together a food parcel and opened the door.

Bowing his head against the wind and rain, Nicu hurried up the lane to the house. By now it was midnight, and there was no doubt the family was sleeping. But the address had led to this place, and though he had never been here before, it was obvious that the family was in need. Reaching out, he knocked on the door.

When it opened, he could just make out the dark shape of a man standing there. "Good evening, sir," Nicu said, smiling. "I know it's late, but I've come to give you some food to eat."

"Oh, how wonderful!" Striking a match, the man held up a candle. The flickering light cast shadows across a face that was lighting up with inexpressible joy. He spoke again, but Nicu hardly heard him. The small house apparently had one room, for a little head had popped up from the floor nearby. More heads were popping up now, gazing toward their midnight visitor with interest. Nicu felt the air leave his lungs as he counted them.

"You have thirteen children?" he asked, turning to the father. At his nod, Nicu said, "Wait here. I'll be right back."

Turning, he dashed out again, running up the hill through the rain toward the camper. His fingers flew as he put together another food parcel and hurried back to the house. "Here's another box of food for your family, sir," he said, handing it to the father at the door.

Tears welled up in the father's eyes. "Thank you," he managed. It was all he could say, but Nicu understood.

Gripping his hand in farewell, Nicu said softly, "There is Someone who always watches over us. We are not alone in this world. May God's blessing be upon you and your family."

It was late December. Snow fell in gentle drifts, settling over the land like a pure white blanket. The sky was a pale, wintry blue, and the sun did little to warm the frigid air.

Nicu drove the camper into a lane that sloped downward, careful to keep his speed low as he steered around the curve. In Germany they had received a package to take to a Romanian family, and they were now stopping to deliver it. But his tires spun on the slick snow, and he had to slow to a crawl. Finally the camper reached its destination safely, and he was able to park.

His passengers got out and walked with him toward the house. Halfway there, Nicu halted. "It sounds as though someone is in the barn, doesn't it?"

The others were silent, listening. There were indeed voices coming from within the barn. Nicu started walking again, leading the way toward the barn.

"Hello!" he called out, pushing the door open slowly. He wondered if anyone heard. The barn was a beehive of activity, and people seemed to be everywhere at once. Nicu saw at a glance what was going on. The family was butchering a pig, like most Romanians did at this time of the year. They would use the meat for their meal on Christmas Day.

Clearing his throat, he raised his voice. "Hello!"

This time the father heard Nicu. He turned sharply, surprise filling his face as he looked at the small group in the doorway of his barn. Nicu stepped forward. "We have come to give you some food, sir," he said, holding up the package in his hand.

The father's face lit with a smile. Washing his hands, he came forward. "We thank you for coming!"

"You're welcome." Smiling, Nicu gestured toward the butchering table. "Are you going to prepare this pig meat for your Christmas dinner?"

"That's what we're planning." The man grinned and gestured toward his wife, who had also come forward. "She cooks delicious meals." The little round lady smiled and blushed.

"We always had pork for Christmas dinner when I was a boy," Nicu said, his voice soft.

The man's wife beamed, her dimples showing. "You must stay and let us cook a meal for you with this meat." Nicu began to protest, but she added, "I won't take no for an answer! We're so happy to have you as guests."

She bustled away then, heading toward the house. Two girls, casting shy glances at the visitors, followed her, leaving the man and his sons alone with their guests. It didn't take long for them to clean up and invite Nicu and his companions into the house. The delicious aroma of the fresh meat, already frying in the pan, greeted them as they opened the door.

Evening was falling by the time they gathered around the table. Nicu asked if he could pray the blessing on the meal, and the father gladly granted his request. As they shared laughter and fellowship, a warm glow seemed to surround the kitchen. Though it wasn't Christmas yet, the season's cheer and goodwill was already descending upon their hearts.

The visitors sang a Christmas carol before they left. As their voices rang in the stillness of the kitchen, Nicu couldn't help thinking of Christmases gone by. This brought back memories of caroling as a child, and later as a youth. There was a sacred beauty in celebrating this time of the year, remembering the Baby who had come to earth thousands of years ago to bring salvation and peace to mankind.

For God so loved the world, that he gave his only begotten Son, that whosoever believeth in him should not perish, but have everlasting life. As he pondered the familiar verse, Nicu felt Christ's holy love surround him with a comforting presence. Salvation was available for anyone who chose to receive it, and he was thankful to be a follower of the King who would reign forever.

31

"All Things Work Together"

Howling winds whipped around the motor home as it plowed through the heavy snow. In the mountains of Vatra Dornei, the snow was deep and the temperature down to -36 degrees Fahrenheit. Nicu was driving almost at a crawl, keeping a wary eye on the diesel fuel gauge at the same time. It was running low, and at 4:00 in the morning, it wouldn't be easy to find help if things took a turn for the worse.

A large form appeared out of the snowy darkness, silhouetted for a moment in the glare of the headlights. In another bound, the deer was directly in front of them. At the impact of the collision, the slow-moving vehicle slid into the ditch.

They shuddered to a halt, and Nicu pressed the gas pedal. Again and again the tires spun, getting them nowhere. And then disaster struck. The motor home coughed and died as the last of its diesel was used up.

"We're stuck here," Nicu said, turning in his seat. "The village of Vatra Dornei isn't too far away. Two of us can walk there while one stays here, and we'll try to call for help."

Nicu set out with one of the boys while the other stayed behind. It was a frigid walk to the phone booth, and they were both shivering violently by the time they reached it. Taking out a coin, Nicu deposited it into the top of the telephone. But it froze where it landed.

Now what? Obviously he couldn't call anyone, and they would have to find another way to get out of the ditch. "Let's try to find some diesel," he decided. "We'll at least be able to restart the vehicle if we find some."

It wasn't a problem to find a can of diesel. But by the time they reached the motor home again, the diesel had frozen, and the vehicle would not start. "Let's take out the fuel pump," Nicu directed. "We'll thaw the diesel and pour it directly into the pump. Maybe then we can get somewhere."

The plan was a good one. With diesel in the pump, they were able to restart the motor home; then Nicu and one of the boys took up positions at the back of the vehicle.

As they pushed with all their strength, the motor home moved forward inch by inch, helped along by the driver pushing the pedal. At last it spun out onto the road again, stopping in a shower of snow that drifted away like white dust.

"Praise the Lord!" Nicu exclaimed as he took his position in the driver's seat again. "He has brought us out once again. Let's thank Him right here before we go on."

In spite of the frigid weather, their hearts were warmed as they realized once again that Someone had been looking out for them on their journey.

Winter faded into the spring of 1989, melting the snow and bringing warm, gentle breezes. Exquisite poppies bloomed, weaving scarlet threads through the grass beside the road. But Nicu hardly noticed the new life around him as he stepped out of the mission and closed the door. For a moment he stood there, gazing at nothing, hearing the words again: "Will you take this printer across the border?"

It was getting more dangerous to smuggle Bibles into Romania; the government was reinforcing its restrictions. The printer, Peter had explained, was to help Romanians print their own Bibles. But it would have to be

"ALL THINGS WORK TOGETHER"

smuggled over the border first.

Nicu's thoughts churned as he drove home. The printer was a massive piece of machinery. There was no place to hide it. What was he going to do?

"I don't have enough faith to take it," he admitted to Monica that night.

She was optimistic about it. "We'll pray for God to give you faith. He will not fail you in this."

But the knowledge of his lack of faith weighed on Nicu's spirit. God was not limited; he knew that. But he wanted to feel completely free of doubt before he took the printer into Romania. He wanted the faith portrayed in 1 John 5:4. "For whatsoever is born of God overcometh the world: and this is the victory that overcometh the world, even our faith."

Nicu stared down at the words, that insurmountable problem rising before him again. There was no place to hide the printer in the motor home. Absolutely none. And he knew that until he felt completely confident in God's omnipotence, he would not consent to take it.

Budapest, the Hungarian capital, was a large and beautiful city. Nicu steered over a bridge, trying to ignore the heaviness of his eyelids. He had been driving all night, but he knew he had to stay awake. The many streets made it difficult to drive.

As they left the city, Nicu knew he could not keep driving much longer. Three people were riding with him, as usual; perhaps one of them could drive. Two people were sleeping, but Marcel's wife Sanda was currently in the passenger seat, staying awake. "Would you drive for me?"

She took one look at his weary face and nodded. "Of course I will."

"Thank you." Pulling off the road, Nicu slid out of the driver's seat and exchanged places with Sanda. As she merged the camper into traffic again, he leaned his head against the seat and fell asleep instantly.

Sanda stepped on the brake as she came up behind a truck. She had already pulled out to pass when she noticed the vehicles coming toward them from the front. She sped up, hoping to pass the truck and get back to her side.

But the truck sped up too. As Sanda passed him and tried to return to her lane, she was not quite far enough ahead. Their vehicles collided. Nicu was jerked awake, the world spinning around him as the camper fell on its side in the street, cutting off the flow of traffic.

For a moment the camper was completely silent. Nicu sat stunned, aware that they were tilting at a crazy angle and that food packages from the shelves above had fallen over him. He reached down to rub his stinging knee. What had happened? Then he heard people rushing to help them.

Still dazed, Nicu got out with the others and stood to one side, watching as the Hungarians tried to lift the camper upright. They seemed to be everywhere, shouting and calling to each other, struggling to lift the camper with their hands. Then someone called out what must have been an order, for everyone stopped what they were doing and took up positions. Another order was called, and in seconds they were all working together, straining to lift until finally the motor home was in an upright position again.

The truck driver had also been standing aside, watching. He turned to Nicu. "Do you want to call the police about this?"

Nicu shook his head. Part of the camper was damaged, but they were safe and still able to drive. "I'm okay with going on if you are."

They talked a few minutes longer and then parted ways. Nicu slid back into the driver's seat, knowing Sanda was too shaken to drive. But he didn't mind; the experience had been enough to keep him awake for a while.

They reached the Romanian border by nightfall. "What happened to your vehicle?" the guard asked, gesturing toward the damaged part of the vehicle.

Nicu explained what had happened. By now the customs officer who controlled the vehicles had also approached. They exchanged glances and seemed to come to an agreement. "We won't search you this time," the

"ALL THINGS WORK TOGETHER"

customs officer said, motioning with one hand. "You're free to go into Romania."

Had they felt sorry for him because of the wrecked vehicle? Nicu wasn't sure, but he was grateful. He stepped gingerly on the pedal, wondering if this was a trick. But no one was stopping him; they were beyond the border now and entering the country of Romania. He drove a distance before stopping in a dark field to open the secret compartments. Had they been opened and damaged as well from the collision? But no; only the food from the shelves had fallen. He bowed his head in a silent prayer of gratitude and then took out the addresses.

Four days later they started home, leaving Romania at a different border crossing. And once again, when the guards saw the damaged motor home, they were merciful and let them go through without a search. As they entered the beautiful country of Austria, Nicu recited his favorite Bible passage aloud to his fellow passengers. " 'And we know that all things work together for good to them that love God . . .' "

The others were silent, realizing the truth in the familiar words. God truly did have ways of working all things together for good—even through a crash that had damaged their motor home.

32

The Longest Trip

"My dear, are you sure about this?"

Monica's voice was soft, her eyes dark with concern. Benjamin and Daniel were spending the evening with friends, and the house was quiet. Twilight filtered through the window panes as she and Nicu stood together by the door.

"I know you never turn anything down," Monica went on. "But this is going to be the longest trip you've ever taken." The shipment of food that Nicu was planning to deliver on this trip was not from Christian Aid for Romania, but from another American mission.

"I figure it'll take three and a half days to get there," Nicu said. "And it will indeed be the longest trip I've ever taken—3,900 kilometers." No doubt he would be driving most of the time. But he didn't mention that.

Monica was studying his face. "You're going to lose a lot of sleep."

He smiled a little. "I always lose sleep on my trips, *schatz*. That's nothing new."

"But—" She bit her lip and looked away. "I must trust you into God's hands," she said quietly, almost to herself. "He has a plan in this."

"Of that I have no doubt." Nicu drew his wife close. "And with you and the boys praying for me while I'm gone, everything will be all right."

But as he closed the door minutes later, Nicu wished the trip would already be over.

The city of Constanța, Romania, was where the American mission had asked Nicu to deliver for them. It was on the far eastern side of Romania. The small group also stopped to deliver Christian literature and food in other areas—Galați, Brăila, and Bucharest. On and on Nicu drove, intent on completing his work and returning home.

After the first several days, the trip began to blur into an endless maze of activity, stopping in city after city to deliver food and Christian literature. And driving—always driving. Nicu's eyes grew heavier, and the road became narrower. Still he drove, a heaviness descending over his spirit and numbness spreading slowly throughout his body. He couldn't even feel his legs anymore. Oh, nothing would feel better than a soft pillow . . . a warm, cozy bed to sleep in . . .

Nicu's eyes flew open. He had fallen asleep! For only a moment, though. The camper was still on the right course. He took a deep breath and knew he was going to have to work harder to stay awake.

He glanced upward. Stars were shining in the balmy summer sky, and the motor home was silent as his passengers slept. Gripping the steering wheel with both hands, Nicu concentrated on the road ahead. He felt he had to stay awake—he was too near home to fall asleep now. All the food and literature had been delivered, and he would soon . . . his thoughts blurred again, and he made a valiant effort to snap out of it. But it was of no use. He was . . . simply . . . too tired . . .

This time the camper careened dangerously close to the edge of the road. Nicu jerked the steering wheel, the action causing his senses to stir to life again. He *must* stay awake.

But the longest trip had taken its toll. When he arrived home, Nicu went directly to the hospital.

Monica stood at Nicu's bedside, watching her husband sleep. Light streamed through the hospital window, sharply defining the extreme weariness in his features. From time to time, the doctor had awakened Nicu for tests. So far the tests had shown nothing.

The door opened behind her, and the doctor came in. "How is our patient this morning?" he asked, pausing by the bed.

"Better, I think. I hope."

Bending over Nicu, the doctor shook his shoulder. "We need to do some more tests."

Nicu stirred and opened his eyes, his gaze settling first on the doctor and then on Monica. She smiled, and he managed a faint smile in return. "Why am I sleeping so much, doctor?" he asked.

"You're making up for lost sleep," the doctor answered simply. He squeezed Nicu's shoulder. "This is the sixth day you've been here, and we're going to keep you as long as necessary."

Nicu fell silent, a faraway look in his eyes. He did not speak again until the door had closed behind the doctor. Then he motioned Monica closer. "One of the boys who traveled with me to Constanța came to visit me last night," he said quietly. "He told me that in each place where we stopped and unloaded literature and food on our trip, the police came and confiscated it all after we left. In one night the police collected everything we delivered, except in Bucharest."

"Oh, no!" Monica gasped.

That faraway look was still in his eyes. "I can't understand why they didn't stop us and search us."

Reaching out, she squeezed his hand. "God protected you."

A smile touched his lips, but he didn't answer; his eyes were already closing again. She sat down on the chair next to the bed as he drifted back to sleep.

The tests continued to show nothing seriously wrong with Nicu, but it was obvious that his nervous system had suffered a breakdown from the constant strain of his lifestyle. Even so, Nicu knew he would not be stopped. He rested deeply in the hospital, and he could feel himself getting stronger every day.

On the ninth day of his stay in the hospital, Nicu answered a knock on the door. "Come in!"

The door opened and his friend Marcel stepped into the room, smiling. "Nicu? How are you this morning?"

"I'm feeling better." Nicu smiled back. "The doctor says I should be able to go home soon."

"Wonderful!" Marcel's smile broadened. "You had a rough trip this last time."

Nicu gestured toward the chair beside his bed. "Sit down, Marcel. Tell me what's been happening these past few days."

"Well, several of us have been buying food and loading the motor home for the next trip into Romania." Marcel gave him a quick glance. "In fact, we brought it here today."

"The motor home?"

"Yes. We were wondering if you would come and close the secret compartments inside. We can bring the camper into the hospital yard."

Nicu smiled. "Sure, Marcel. I'll come down and close them."

The following day Nicu was released from the hospital, and he soon embarked on his next trip to Romania.

Nicu and his helpers traveled 1,100 kilometers to Reşiţa, Romania. With the others taking turns driving, Nicu was able to rest. "We're supposed to give some medicine to a brother from the church here," Marcel said to Nicu as he turned into a gate. The lawn was well-kept, and flowers bloomed beside the house.

Nicu opened the passenger's door. "Perhaps I can give him some literature too."

The brother was already waiting at the door. "Hello," Nicu said politely, reaching out to shake his hand. "We're here to give you some medicine."

The man squinted in the sunlight, his voice gruff. "It's about time. We've been waiting on that medicine for days. I was almost ready to make another call."

Nicu stepped back. "Well, we're here now, sir," he said, keeping his smile intact. "I'll give the medicine to you in a minute."

Without waiting for an answer, he headed back to the motor home. "We won't give any literature here," he whispered to Marcel as he stepped into the back. "We'll just give the medicine and go on." The impression deep within him was one he often sensed—a feeling from God that told him whether the people he spoke with were true followers of Christ or not.

Taking the medicine from the shelf, Nicu gave it to the church member and wished him a good day. Then he climbed back into the motor home, and they drove away.

33

God's Secret Agent

"Did you smuggle the printer into Romania?"

It had become the mission's standard question as the months passed by. Nicu always had to shake his head. "I didn't have enough faith to take it. There's no place to hide it in the camper," was the only answer he had to give.

"Don't worry," they assured him. "We'll continue to pray."

Nicu thought about their words now as he rolled down his window for the border patrol officer. Early autumn breezes touched his face. After visiting his mother, he had traveled to the border of Oradea, the one he used most whenever he left Romania. He would be heading into Yugoslavia from here.

"I need to see your passport, please." The officer held out his hand.

"Yes, sir."

"Your name?"

"Nicolae Craiovan."

The border officer asked a few more questions before stepping aside to let the customs officer take over. "I want you to take everything from your vehicle," he ordered.

Nicu's passengers joined him in taking out the food packages and placing them on the pavement. Minutes later they stood back as the officer entered the motor home. He glanced around and then turned to Nicu. "Do you have a screwdriver? A Phillips," he specified.

Nicu felt his hands turn cold. He forced himself to meet the officer's gaze. "I'll look in my tools to see if I have it." But he already knew the screwdriver would be there. He had it along for every trip he took into Romania.

"If you don't have it, I can find one," the officer said.

Nicu opened the lid of the tool box, hoping the officer wouldn't see his hands shaking. "Yes," he said finally. "I have one here."

The officer took it and turned away, heading directly toward the secret compartments in the motor home. Climbing up on a bench, he began to loosen the first screw.

Nicu stood frozen, his eyes riveted on the officer as he finished loosening the first screw and started on the second one below it. There were twelve screws in all on this secret compartment—six on the top and six on the bottom. It seemed like only a second before the officer finished the second screw and reached up to the loosen the third.

He obviously suspected something, or else he wouldn't be loosening those screws. By now he was working on the fifth screw. Nicu's heart stopped, and then began to race as the officer loosened the sixth one. His secret was going to be discovered.

Turning away, he stood with his back to the officer. *Lord, please, stop him now!* As the desperate cry of his heart winged its way heavenward, he felt a tap on his shoulder.

"You can have this back." The officer had come down from the bench and was standing behind him, holding up the screwdriver. "You are free to go."

We'll continue to pray. The words the mission brothers had spoken came to Nicu's mind as he stared down at the screwdriver in his hand. He knew now beyond the shadow of a doubt that the God who could change a hardened officer's mind in a heartbeat was more than able to take the printer safely across the border.

"This is all I can do." Nicu stepped back to survey his work. Monica and the boys stood with him, the silence hanging over them so thick he could almost feel it.

"I now feel free to take the printer into Romania," Nicu had told the brothers at the mission. It was the beginning of November, and the weather was cold. Snow flurries whitened the air outside the motor home as the family studied the object that could cost their beloved one's life.

The box into which Nicu had packed the printer was extremely large. He had broken some of the food packages for the trip and scattered sugar and rice over the top of the printer. If it were opened, this would be the first thing that was seen; perhaps the officials would think that the whole box was filled with food and let it go.

Now the boxed printer was resting on top of the stove in the motor home. The people at the mission had assured Nicu that they would continue to pray, and he knew Monica and the boys would pray as well. As he looked at the box, large as life in plain sight, Nicu marveled at the peace he felt deep within.

"I believe God is going to give us the victory," he said, glancing at Monica.

For a moment he thought she wasn't going to answer. But when she finally looked up, there was a soft light in her eyes. "Your faith is strong, dear." She slipped her hand into his. "And isn't faith the victory that overcomes the world?"

"Indeed, it is! This printer is in God's hands, and I believe He'll see us through." He reached out to Benjamin and Daniel with the other hand. "Come closer, boys. Let's pray together before I leave."

Nicu drove through the scenic countryside of Austria and on into Hungary. Vivid sunset colors were painting the western sky when he pulled off to one side of the road and stopped. "We have six hundred kilometers to go until we reach the border of Romania," he said, turning in his seat. "I want to pray here." His passengers nodded silently, already bowing their heads.

But Nicu had a special request this time. "Since I've been going to Romania so often, I know all the guards," he said quietly. "Most times I can calculate who's on duty. But tonight I want to pray specifically that two certain guards will not be on duty. One is a customs officer who searches vehicles, and the other is a border officer who has authority over all the guards. They are rougher than any of the others, and I don't want them to be there."

As they prayed aloud one by one, Nicu remembered his words to Monica. *God will give us the victory.* He believed it with all his heart; but when they reached the border, his courage took the first plunge. The customs officer who searched the vehicles was absent, but the border officer who had the highest authority immediately approached his vehicle. Nicu groaned inwardly as he rolled down the window. *Oh, Lord, why did you let this happen? You know I have to take this printer into Romania.*

"Good morning, Craiovan." The border officer gave him a stiff salute as he approached the window.

"Good morning," Nicu answered calmly.

Now that the officer was up close, Nicu could see the flash in his eyes and the tightness of his lips. The man was even more agitated than usual, his voice hard as steel. "Craiovan, I'm going to search you today like I never did before," he said abruptly. "Do you have guns? Pornography? Bibles?"

Nicu gestured toward the dash, where his Bible was lying as usual. "My Bible is here."

Turning, the border officer barked an order to the customs officer on duty. "Take everything out of their vehicle and search them."

Unloading the food was quite a task. The packages were everywhere—in drawers, on the benches, and in every corner. The customs officer put them all in the center of the vehicle, where they made a large pile.

But the boxed printer on the stove—that massive box in plain sight—was never touched. Nicu, praying silently the whole time the officer searched, grew more and more tense. The customs officer went to the back of the camper and opened the door. Did he not see the box even from there? He certainly wasn't mentioning it.

At last the customs officer stepped back and looked all around. Nicu held his breath. Surely now he would see that box—surely now his secret would be discovered.

The customs officer turned to his higher authority. "I'm finished with the search, sir."

An angry flush crept up the border officer's neck. "You didn't find anything?"

"Only what he usually transports—food."

The officer spun on his heel, his eyes flashing as he stalked toward Nicu. His boot stomped down heavily on the camper's step, the sound reverberating through the night. "I'm sure you have something in this camper!"

Nicu held out one hand. "Please search again."

The border officer wasted no time in reentering the camper. He paced the interior, his gaze raking the empty spaces where the other guard had unloaded the food packages. He bent down, rifling through the large pile in the center of the floor. He walked right past the immense box on the stove without touching it, coming at last to the door again.

"Give me what you have for me, and I'm finished."

Had he heard correctly? The officer hadn't found anything? Forcing himself to remain calm, Nicu handed over the gift and stood still, watching the officer walk away. They were truly free to go! He wanted to shout and sing for joy, but instead joined the others in replacing the food packages.

At last they left the border, their hearts overflowing with praise to the

God who was able to do exceedingly more than anything they ever asked or thought. He had performed an amazing miracle, blinding the eyes of the officers and bringing the printer safely across the border into Romania.

"I always ask God to help me in my work," Nicu shared with the others. "Sometimes I see a solution my way, but God works it out differently. Later I can see that God's way was perfect."

As Nicu pondered his calling and God's protection, he realized that he was a secret agent for God, called to work undercover for His kingdom. He was secure in the hands of the Supreme Being whose ways were infinitely higher than his own.

34

The Organ

Dancing sunbeams and merry birdsong enhanced the clear summer air. Butterflies hovered over flowers in full bloom, and from the lawn next door came the sound of laughter as Benjamin and Daniel played soccer with their friends.

From where they sat on the porch sipping their coffee, Nicu and Monica could watch the game. "Our boys are growing up, aren't they?" Nicu remarked.

Monica smiled. "They'll be on their own before we know it." She gave him a questioning glance. "Was Renata ever able to buy an organ for the church in Deva?"

Nicu shook his head. "She talked with an organization who offered to sell her an electronic organ for 45,000 German marks. We don't have nearly that much money!" The church in the Romanian village of Deva needed an organ, and Nicu had said he would try to provide one for them. "After some negotiation, they agreed to let us have it for 10,000 marks," he went on. "Renata ordered it, but I'm not sure what we're going to do about the payment."

Monica glanced across the lawn, watching the boys' game for a moment. "Perhaps you could announce the need in church and ask everyone to pray that God will give us the money," she suggested.

"That's a good idea. I'll do it in the service tonight."

But even after Nicu announced the need, very few people gave money. "The deadline for buying the organ is coming up fast, and I'm planning to go to Romania next week," he said one evening as the family sat down at the supper table. "We still need 1,000 marks to pay for the organ. If we don't get that money soon . . ." His voice trailed off.

"There's still time," Monica said reassuringly.

"God has always come through for you before, hasn't He?" Benjamin piped up. "He knows the need."

Nicu smiled. "Thanks, son. I needed that reminder."

Twilight was stealing across the land as church members visited outside the church. "You're leaving tomorrow for Romania, aren't you?" Robert asked as he shook Nicu's hand.

Nicu nodded. "My family and a few other youth are planning to go along."

"Do you have enough money yet to pay for that organ?"

"I'm afraid not," Nicu admitted. "We've waited and waited, but nothing has happened. Perhaps God has something different in mind for the church in Deva."

"Deva? That's where the police always follow you, isn't it?" An older brother named Richard had joined them, coming up just in time to hear the last of their conversation.

"They often do," Nicu said. "I'm never able to distribute much there."

They visited a few minutes longer, and then Richard changed the subject. "I'm almost ready to leave, but I have something to give you, Nicu." Reaching into his pocket, he pulled out an envelope and handed it to Nicu. "May God help you on your trip tomorrow!"

"Thanks, and God bless you." Nicu waved goodbye, pocketing the envelope as he turned back to Robert. His curiosity was piqued, but he waited to open the envelope until his family was in the car, ready to leave church.

"Look at this!" His exclamation brought every head up. "It's money—1,000 marks!" He held it up for Monica and the boys to see, his eyes shining with excitement. "Richard was gone the night I announced our need for money—he didn't know about it. But he gave this tonight—exactly the amount we need to pay for the organ!"

"Oh, that's amazing!" Monica's smile lit her face, and the boys studied the money with wide eyes.

"Is it real?" Daniel breathed.

Nicu and Monica laughed. "I can hardly believe it myself," Nicu admitted. "I was giving up on this money ever coming. But it did come—right at the last minute."

"There's nothing that says God can't wait until the last minute, is there?" Monica was still beaming.

"Absolutely not." Nicu placed the money back in the envelope and started the engine. "But really," he added more seriously, "God didn't wait until the last minute—He was right on time."

The trip to Deva passed without invasion by the secret police. In three days they had started for home, traveling through the night. Monica rode up front with Nicu while the other passengers slept.

The clock was showing 11:30 p.m. when they heard over the news that a large vehicle was moving in their direction, driving erratically. "That sounds dangerous," Nicu said, activating his turn signal. "I should probably pull this motor home off the road since it takes up so much space."

Only minutes later, headlights pierced the darkness as a vehicle barreled down upon them, never slowing as it whooshed past. Nicu sucked in his breath, his hands tightening on the steering wheel. "Someone's going to get hurt if he keeps driving like that!"

Monica glanced in the rearview mirror. "The car is already out of sight," she noted.

They might have forgotten about the incident if they hadn't heard later what happened. "Did you hear the news, Monica?" Nicu asked, striding into the kitchen. "There was a big accident in the area where we were driving that night we were coming home from Romania."

Monica's hand flew over her heart. "If we hadn't moved over when we did—"

"The Lord protected us," he said simply.

Her gaze was still on his face. "You know . . . have you ever stopped and thought about how much God has done for you? And I don't mean just in your travels," she added. "Throughout your entire life, God has been preparing you for what you do now."

Nicu cocked his head, silently considering Monica's words. Smuggling Bibles and delivering food for Christian Aid for Romania was his life—he simply did what God asked him to do. At home he was kept busy as a leader in two different churches—the Romanian church he had founded and also a German church.

But now his wife had helped him to realize anew that God had indeed been working in his life from the beginning, preparing him for this work. Even in the trying times when he couldn't understand, God had seen the whole picture and orchestrated everything to fit into His perfect design.

Standing there at the counter, Nicu bowed his head and silently thanked God for keeping him in the center of His will.

35

"You Must Go Back"

"Would you like to go with us to Romania, Elena?" Nicu set down his coffee cup, glancing across the table at their visitor. "I bought food for another trip, and I plan to pack the camper tomorrow."

Elena Boghian's eyes shone as she glanced up. "I haven't been to Romania in six years. It would be so nice to see my family!" It was November of 1989. As Nicu's contact for Christian Aid for Romania, Elena had come to Germany to see how things were going with his work. Now they were having their evening meal. A chilly wind sent crisp autumn leaves skittering across the lawn outside, but inside it was warm and cozy.

"There are several other people going along," Nicu explained. "We'll drive most of the night."

They started out the next evening, traveling through Germany toward Austria. Ancient castles built on hilltops stood silhouetted against the sunset sky, and villages lit up the countryside as twilight stole across it. The moon rose, casting a silvery scarf over snow-peaked mountains. Nicu did most of the driving through the long hours of the night, trading now and then with the other man in the vehicle.

They reached the border at dawn. Nicu stopped and rolled down his window as the guard approached and announced, "I want to see your passports."

Nicu handed his over, watching as the guard collected all the other passports. When the guard had disappeared into his office, Elena spoke quietly. "I have an American passport. It won't be a problem for me to enter Romania, will it? I am an American citizen now."

"I don't know why there would be a problem," answered Nicu. But they waited and waited, and still the guard did not return. The sun had risen higher, doing its best to ward off the chill in the air, when the guard finally stepped out of his office.

"Take everything from your vehicle, Craiovan," he ordered.

The others joined him in unloading everything from the camper. Then they stood off to one side as the guards searched. The minutes crept by, and finally the guards disappeared, leaving everything where it was.

Now what? They had already been waiting for a long time, and now they had to wait again. And wait. And wait. The food packages were still scattered over the pavement. Why wasn't the officer returning?

At long last the officer came toward them. "Put everything back," he said, his voice clipped. "Do a U-turn and go back. You are not allowed to enter Romania."

Nicu stood stunned. "Why?" he asked slowly.

Hot color crept into the officer's face. "You must go back," he barked. "Is that clear?"

"Yes, sir." Nicu held out the gift bag he had prepared for the guard. "Won't you take this?"

The guard shook his head. "Put everything back," he repeated. Without waiting for an answer, he turned and strode away.

"I'm sorry," Nicu said to Elena as they repacked the motor home. "I know you were excited about seeing your mother and siblings again."

"I could hardly wait," she answered, trying to smile. "But this isn't your fault. I'm sure it had something to do with my passport."

They stopped in Hungary on the way back to Germany, unloading some of the food at a Christian home. Elena left for the United States soon after that, already good friends with the Craiovan family.

"Come in!" Nicu met the pastor and his wife at the door, smiling broadly. "It's not often we get visitors from California."

The pastor laughed as they shook hands. "We're looking forward to spending time with you."

"Welcome!" Monica came to the kitchen doorway, her sweet smile lighting her face. "The meal is almost ready, so you can all go to the table."

Benjamin and Daniel were already there, standing behind their chairs. The others took their positions, and Nicu led in prayer.

"You have plans to visit Romania after you leave here, don't you?" Nicu asked after they sat down.

The pastor nodded. "Could you help us rent a motor home to go there?"

"That's no problem," Nicu assured him. He spread a slice of bread with butter, adding cheese on top. "I often take food into Romania, but on my last trip we weren't able to enter. So we had a lot of food left over." He glanced up, meeting the pastor's gaze. "Would you be willing to take it into Romania with you? Some of the food could also be delivered in Hungary."

"We can do that," the pastor responded instantly.

"I'll provide you with the addresses," Nicu went on.

"We'd be very happy to do it," the pastor's wife said softly. "We've heard much about Romania's poverty, and we would be glad to do what we can."

"Will things ever change over there?" the pastor asked.

Nicu shook his head. "I don't know. President Ceaușescu is almost killing the Romanians."

He said nothing more, and the conversation soon drifted to other things. But the question stayed with Nicu—what did the future hold for Romania? If things didn't change, the country was headed for ruin.

But God was still in control. He knew all about the situation, and they could entrust it into His hands. There was no need to fear the future, for God was already there.

36

The Revolution

Nicu slid out of the driver's seat of the motor home, shivering in the onslaught of the frigid December air. He glanced at his watch and saw that it was 11:00 p.m. Now he searched the crowds. He had a package for an elderly lady from her daughter who lived in Nuremberg. Even at this hour, the big square in Timişoara was bustling with activity.

In the next instant he saw her—a lady leaning on a cane, hobbling toward him. Nicu strode forward, reaching out to shake her hand. "Hello!" After chatting for a minute, he said, "I'll take this package to your house for you."

She shook her head, looking slightly nervous. "That isn't necessary."

"I'll take it," Nicu insisted. "Please allow me."

The lady shook her head again, the streetlights glinting on her snowy hair. Nicu hesitated. She wasn't explaining why she refused his help; perhaps she would give in if he tried one more time. But she was adamant. "No, no, no! I appreciate you coming, but I can take it home myself."

"Okay," Nicu said at last. "Good night." Climbing back into the camper, he revved the engine to life. "She didn't accept my help," he said in a low tone to Marcel who was riding in the passenger's seat.

Marcel was studying the crowded square. "Quite a few policemen went by a few minutes ago. Is something going on here?"

"If she knew about the police, she didn't tell me." Nicu turned onto a side street, heading out of the city. In two hours he could cross the border and be in Hungary. On and on he drove through the moonlit night.

They had crossed the border and were traveling through Hungary when they heard the news. The border of Romania was on lockdown. No one could go in, and no one could go out.

Nicu and Marcel looked at each other. "Something must have happened since we left," Nicu said. "But what?"

It wasn't until he reached home that Nicu learned the truth. The president of Romania and his wife had disappeared, trying to escape assassination at the hands of their own people. "The border was closed so that the president couldn't get out," Nicu realized. "I'd say this is only the beginning of some radical changes for Romania."

"Do you think the lady knew what was happening that night you met her in the square?" Monica asked.

"She could have. I offered to take the package to her house, but she didn't want me to go with her. She probably felt the danger." Nicu paused. Then he looked at his wife steadily. "I'm planning to fill the camper today to go back to Romania. I'll be taking food parcels as well as medicines for a hospital."

Her face turned white. "It's only been three days since you came home, Nicu. And it's too dangerous to go back!"

"I have a work to do there," he reminded her quietly. "I'll be traveling with God."

On Sunday, December 17, Nicu announced to the church that he was going back to Romania. A hush fell over the congregation, and Nicu read concern in many faces. They all knew what was happening in Romania. Things would likely get worse before they got better.

There was a new earnestness in the prayers of the believers as they came before God, asking His protection over Nicu. They prayed for Monica and the boys who would be staying at home. They prayed for the situation in Romania, committing it to the control of their Father's hands. As

THE REVOLUTION

he listened to the saints praying, peace settled over Nicu's spirit. He didn't know what the coming days held, but their prayers would follow him.

After trying to make their escape in a helicopter, the president of Romania and his wife were caught on December 22, and the borders opened again. Nicu, already waiting at the border near Timişoara, drew a breath of relief when the guards let him through without a problem. "They don't know me so well here," he remarked to Aaron. His friend from church rode in the passenger's seat, with his trailer hooked to the back of the motor home.

Aaron's expression was sober. "Nicu, I feel uneasy," he confessed in a low tone. "I know that people at home are praying for us, but I feel as if we're headed into trouble."

Nicu gave him an understanding glance but didn't say anything. Much as he wanted to deny it, he felt the same way. They had reached the city's limit by now. At 6:00 in the evening, the streets were jammed with people, and soldiers with guns appeared throughout the city. Nicu had never seen such a sight. He slowed the camper to a crawl, but even so, he had to stop every ten meters for an officer to check him out and make sure he wasn't a terrorist.

"The revolution has begun," Nicu said tensely to Aaron as he rolled up his window for the fifteenth time. "The fighting started in Timişoara, and it's spreading. And we're right in the middle of it. If we can reach the church where we're supposed to deliver the food parcels, we'll be able to get off the streets. But until then . . ." His voice trailed off. Gripping the steering wheel with both hands, he searched the street ahead. At this rate they were hardly getting anywhere.

One hour dragged by. Then another. A wide band of rich, vivid pink hued the western sky as the sun went down, but its beauty seemed out of place in this chaos. The sunset faded into twilight, and still they inched along the street, trying to reach the church where they could be secure behind the gates. All the while, soldiers and people were everywhere.

The clock was showing 10:00 p.m. when Nicu stepped on the brakes again and opened his window for yet another officer. He answered the officer's questions, returning them with a request of his own. "Sir, will you come with us in the camper and help us get to the church? I have the address for it right here. We are planning to deliver medicines for the hospital."

The officer looked at him, then up and down the street. The streetlights shone on his face, revealing a hint of compassion in his eyes when he turned back to Nicu. "I can do that." Walking around to the other side, he opened the door and climbed in.

Nicu stepped on the gas again, and they moved forward. But now another officer was flagging them down. As Nicu stopped and rolled down the window, the officer in the back seat leaned forward. "It's okay," he called out.

After a surprised glance, the officer waved them on. In this way they were able to move faster, with the officer in the back seat directing the way to the church. When at last they arrived, they entered through the church's high gates.

Nicu's brother-in-law Tinu was waiting for them. "The camper will be safe here," Tinu assured them. "You're welcome to come to my apartment for the night."

Nicu and Aaron accepted the offer without hesitation. Thanking the officer for his help, they locked up the camper and walked with Tinu to his apartment. It was emptier on the back streets, and they quickly reached Tinu's home.

Tinu's wife served them a snack while they relaxed in the kitchen. "Tomorrow we're planning to go to the hospital," Nicu said, taking a sip of coffee. "They have contagious diseases there, and we'll be delivering medicines."

His sister-in-law looked troubled. "Be careful. You'll have to cross the city to get there, and on the main street there's a lot of shooting."

THE REVOLUTION

"The building of the security office is on that street," Tinu explained.

Nicu's brow furrowed. "I'm afraid we don't have any other way to the hospital but to go through there."

Tinu clasped his shoulder. "We'll be praying for you."

Nicu lay awake for a long time that night, unable to sleep. The tension of the day had worn him down, and they still weren't out of danger. What did the morrow hold? In the darkness he remembered again his last moments with his family before he had left—how Monica had clung to him as they said goodbye, her heart in her eyes. He could only imagine what she was going through right now as the revolution grew worse. His growing sons had seemed like young men standing with their mother when he had finally opened the door to leave. Would he live to return to them?

He tossed. He turned. At last Nicu sat up and snapped on the light. He reached for his Bible and paged through it, praying silently. He stopped at Psalm 27, his eyes falling on verse 5. "For in the time of trouble he shall hide me in his pavilion: in the secret of his tabernacle shall he hide me; he shall set me up upon a rock."

When Nicu closed the Bible, his heart had calmed with a measure of peace.

Icicles hung from the roof, glittering like crystal gems in the sunlight. Snowdrifts decorated tiled roofs up and down the street. But the morning's beauty was lost on Monica as she rolled over in bed, reaching out to turn off the alarm clock. She let her head drop back on the pillow, stifling a groan. She had hardly been able to sleep at all the past few nights. How could she get up and face yet another nightmarish day?

With every new piece of information she heard about Romania, Monica's fear grew. The revolution was becoming worse and worse, and her husband was in the middle of it. The war was killing and wounding many people. Where was Nicu? Was he still safe? Would he come out of that chaos alive?

The burden on Monica's heart was crushing her. Hideous fears stared her in the face, screaming, *He's wounded! He's dead! He'll never come home!* She prayed desperately for her husband's protection, but felt that she was drowning in a sea of doubt. She knew the church was also praying for him. Would God hear their prayers and spare Nicu's life? Or would He choose to take His secret agent home this time? Never had it been so hard to say, "Thy will be done."

The streets were emptier. Nicu steered the camper carefully, his windows tightly closed. But they could still hear the shooting—a rapid, staccato beat of fire that rained mercilessly on young and old alike. By the time they reached the hospital, Nicu's whole body was tense.

Rolling down his window, Nicu spoke to the officer at the gate. "We have medicines to deliver here, sir."

He nodded. "We'll open the gate for you to enter the hospital yard." Within minutes Nicu had parked the camper in the lawn, and they were ready to go in.

Now that they were in the open air, the sounds of fighting were even clearer. Nicu and Aaron hurried across the lawn, reaching the door behind a young man carrying his mother into the hospital. She was bleeding profusely from a gunshot wound, her eyes closed and her face ashen. Her son was straining under the weight of her body, and it was obvious he couldn't hold out much longer.

Nicu was stepping forward to offer his help when the mother gave one last gasp for breath and slumped in her son's arms. A low cry escaped the boy's lips as he dropped to his knees, his slight frame shaking with sobs. Nicu knelt beside him, taking the woman's hand to feel her pulse. She was gone.

Tears welled in Nicu's eyes as he looked at the prostrate boy weeping over his mother's dead body. How many more people would die before this was all over? Placing an arm around the boy's shoulders, Nicu bowed his head and prayed aloud for him. Aaron also prayed, resting a gentle hand on the boy's head. It was all they could do for the young man.

When they spoke with the chief of the hospital about the medicines, Nicu and Aaron discovered that the rooms were filled with people wounded from the fighting. A doctor took them from room to room, where Nicu stopped at each bed and prayed aloud for the suffering individual. He had no doubt that their wounds went much deeper than physical pain. They had been through much emotional trauma. He could only hope that his prayers would be a source of encouragement to them.

After unloading the medicines for the hospital, Nicu and Aaron headed silently back to Tinu's apartment for the night.

37

"I Have No Chance"

"Here is where it all started. Many people were killed in this square." Nicu stood with Aaron and Tinu at the edge of the large city square, gesturing toward the left. "I met the elderly lady over there with the package and offered to take it home for her, but she didn't want me to."

They were silent for a moment. Then Tinu spoke in a hushed tone. "Over there is the cathedral where a big group of children were killed on the steps when the shooting started."

Nicu followed his gaze. The cathedral was built with amazing architecture, its walls and pillars rising to the sky in majestic splendor. But it had meant death to fifty dear children when they came up the steps, hoping to hide inside the cathedral. The priest had locked the door, and there had been no escape for them.

Just thinking about it brought tears to his eyes. He cleared his throat and spoke huskily. "And . . . we're still alive. Why were we spared when innocent children weren't?"

But it still isn't over. Though Nicu didn't say it aloud, the thought was unsettling. President Ceaușescu was still awaiting his sentence; meanwhile, the revolution went on.

Nicu and Aaron left that afternoon when their work was finished, traveling out of Timișoara toward the border of Hungary. They reached the locality of Becica, heading through the city. As they reached the other side, Nicu slowed the camper to steer around a curve. Glancing ahead, he jerked upright in his seat, his hands freezing on the steering wheel.

Straight before them on the road was a large machine gun, raining unceasing fire into the air. Fifteen civilians with guns were standing around it, waiting to stop and search every vehicle passing through. *I have no chance to get through this!* Beads of sweat formed on Nicu's forehead as he stopped the motor home. The men were coming toward him, surrounding the vehicle on all sides. Nicu opened his window a little and tried to talk to them, but extreme nervousness had warped his tongue. Any one of these stern-faced men could shoot him at any moment.

Then he saw an older man coming toward him. Nicu's breath came faster. He rolled down his window all the way this time, every nerve in his body straining under the effort to appear calm. But his thoughts were anguished. *I might as well talk to him; I have no chance anyway. My life is over. Oh, God . . .*

"We received information that terrorists are coming this way, and we have an order to watch this place." The man's voice was grim as he stopped outside the window. "Do you have any fighters in your vehicle?"

"No, only my friend," Nicu said. "But you may look."

The torturous minutes stretched long, and still they waited while the older man searched. All the while, the other men stood outside with their guns trained on the vehicle, making sure no one was hiding. By the time they received permission to leave, Nicu was exhausted. With everything he had already gone through, this added suspense was almost too much.

At twilight they finally reached the border. As Nicu stopped the motor home, all the border patrol officers came and surrounded them. "Where did you come from?" one asked.

"We came from Timişoara."

"What's happening there?"

"Revolution. Many people are being killed and wounded by the fighting."

As Nicu shared everything he had seen, his pent-up emotions broke loose. Unable to go on, he covered his face and cried uncontrollably, his whole body trembling.

They brought him a glass of water, waiting in respectful silence until the emotional storm passed. Then the customs officer spoke again, his voice kind. "You can go home, Craiovan."

Nicu met his gaze, hardly daring to believe the words. They weren't going to search him?

"You can go home," the officer repeated, smiling a little. There was nothing but sympathy in his tone, and it nearly made Nicu break down again.

Instead, he nodded and squared his shoulders. "Thank you, sir." God surely must have known that this was exactly what he needed.

Home had never looked so wonderful. Monica met him at the door, and for a time no words were spoken as they clung to each other. He felt her shaking against him as he relived those moments of terror when he had been certain his life was over. What if it had truly been the end? He shuddered and held her even closer. Nothing on earth was more precious than his family, and he was so glad to still be with them.

He reveled in seeing his sons again. Benjamin and Daniel had also been praying for him without ceasing while he was gone. The four of them gathered around the table, joining hands while Nicu led in a heartfelt prayer of thanksgiving. They were all keenly aware that Nicu could have been missing.

Nicu shared the depths of his heart with Monica that night after they were alone in their room. "I've seen a lot over these past few days, *schatz*: pain, suffering, and death. When I saw that machine gun, I was certain my own life was over. I thought I'd never see you or the boys again—" His voice broke, and he couldn't finish.

Tears fell unheeded down her cheeks as she buried her face against his shoulder. "Oh, Nicu, I was so afraid . . ." The whispered words were muffled, but he heard them clearly. "You help others, but you don't think about how you would leave a widow and two fatherless sons."

A widow and two fatherless sons. Nicu tried to speak but couldn't. His arms tightened around her, and they wept together. At last he drew back a little, looking deeply into her eyes. "I love you, Monica, and I am thankful to God that He has brought me back home safely to you and our boys."

38

God Is Not Limited

President Ceaușescu and his wife were executed on Christmas Day, 1989. With the borders opened, the way was clear to begin Romanian aid in earnest. On January 3, Nicu sent a load of food from Germany to Romania. He took the rest of the month off work to transport cargo for Christian Aid for Romania. The organization collected many donations and sent them to Rotterdam by ship, where three 40-foot container trucks brought the food parcels into Hungary. Nicu met them there with his motor home and guided them to Romania.

As they reached the familiar border, Nicu marveled at the change in the atmosphere. There was nothing to hide anymore; they were free to enter. He rolled down his window for the guard, who approached him with a smile. "May I see your passport?"

"Yes, sir."

"What are you bringing in?"

"Food parcels and Bibles."

The guard glanced up. "May we have some Bibles?"

Nicu's eyes widened. These guards wanted Bibles? A broad smile broke across his face. "I'd be happy to give you Bibles, sir!"

He handed out ten of the sacred books, still awed by what was happening. Did the guards realize what treasures they were holding? Within those pages were words of life and hope, words that could change their lives. As he watched the guards, Nicu prayed that God would bless their open hearts. This was definitely the crown of his ministry.

Nicu entered Romania ten times in January and February of 1990, driving 50,000 kilometers to deliver Bibles and food parcels. In April, Elena Boghian returned with a group of brothers and sisters from the U.S., meeting Nicu in Hungary. The three of them were to guide three truckloads of goods into Romania.

"We helped ten orphanages with these goods," Nicu told Monica after he returned home. "The situation of those children is terrible."

"Was Elena able to get into Romania this time?"

He nodded and grinned. "The same people who had turned her back earlier now welcomed her with a big smile because we were bringing charity goods." His grin widened. "And that's not all! They also gave us vouchers to get food at a restaurant, gas, and hotels for free. They grant these to anyone who brings charity goods since the war. People from all over are coming to help Romania."

"They don't have anything over there," Monica commented.

"Yes, everything has to come from elsewhere," Nicu agreed. "Houses are being built, and many other things are needed." He paused before changing the subject. *"Schatz,* what would you think about taking a trip to America?"

Her eyes widened. "America?"

"I've been working for Christian Aid for Romania for three years, you know. I would really like to see what goes on behind the scenes."

Monica nodded understandingly. "It would be a good experience. I've always wanted to visit America."

"Isn't it strange?" Nicu remarked. "Back when we escaped from Romania, we really wanted to go to America. But God has been able to do much good for Romania by keeping us here. I wouldn't have been able to do missionary work like this if our plans had worked out."

"God's ways aren't our ways," Monica said thoughtfully.

"He always proves Himself," Nicu said, a faraway look coming into his eyes. "When I took the printer to Romania in November, I could have waited another month. I didn't know the revolution was coming. But God's timing is always perfect."

They were silent for a moment. Then Monica asked softly, "How do you feel now that your smuggling is finished in Romania?"

"I feel like there's a hole in my heart," he admitted. "I can't pray like I used to. I still pray, but the tension isn't there anymore—it isn't the same earnest prayer. The risk, danger, and fear are gone."

"Well, I certainly don't miss that!" Her eyes grew a little moist. "I often had to think of my father's words while you were gone—how we need to give our fears to God. He makes no mistakes." She paused, a faint smile touching her lips. "As hard as it was sometimes, God was always there to carry me through."

Nicu took his wife's hand. "These three years have not been easy, *schatz*, but I thank God that He could use me for something like this." As he spoke, the light in his dark eyes shone brighter than Monica had ever seen it.

"Isn't this amazing?" Nicu paused in his work, glancing over the many busy volunteers filling Christian Aid for Romania's warehouse.

On this day, May 30, 1990, many Amish and Mennonite people had gathered to pack goods for shipments to other countries. "What a tremendous amount of aid comes from here and is shipped through Germany to Romania!"

Monica followed his gaze. "It is amazing," she agreed. "I only wish we could understand each other's languages."

Nicu grinned. "At least we have Elena Boghian and Silvia Tarniceriu to translate." The two Romanian ladies had been present when he had met with Christian Aid for Romania's staff members—David Troyer, Paul Weaver, and others—to discuss how the aid should be handled in Romania. Now that the border was open, they were free to do as they pleased.

"I'll be giving a report on my work tonight, with Silvia translating," Nicu went on. He gazed over the warehouse again. It was deeply touching to see these brothers and sisters who put money together—hundreds of thousands of dollars—to send to him for God's work.

A few days later, Nicu and Monica said goodbye to their new friends and boarded the airliner bound for Germany. "It's good to get to know people from the United States," Nicu said as they waited for takeoff. "I was so touched to see how the Mennonite and Amish brothers and sisters are so faithful."

"So was I," Monica answered softly. "What's going to happen now?"

"Well, I'll be working for Christian Aid for Romania on another basis this year, buying cars and trucks to take into Romania for distributions." He paused, and his voice quieted. "You know, seeing all those people working together made me realize all over again how big God is, and that we can trust in Him."

She smiled. "He is truly a great God."

"There's a Romanian proverb that I had to think about while we were here," Nicu went on. " 'The ones who are alike will gather together.' My work of smuggling wasn't my own endeavor. If it hadn't been for God's children, it couldn't have worked."

They sat in silence for a moment, watching the activity outside the plane window. Then Nicu reached into his backpack, drawing out his Bible. Monica turned to watch as he paged through it, stopping eventually at John 10:16. " 'And other sheep I have, which are not of this fold,' " he read aloud. " 'Them also I must bring, and they shall hear my voice; and there shall be one fold, and one shepherd.' " He glanced up. "When God prepares a work, He brings the people together."

"Even if they are on opposite sides of the ocean," Monica said with a smile.

The joy in Nicu's voice was obvious when he replied, "Yes, God is able to bring together His agents anywhere to accomplish His plan. I don't have to be a secret agent anymore, but He protected me and His work when I was one. And I know that when I can no longer do things for Him, He will be able to make His work go on—even into eternity."

Afterword

In the years following his work with Christian Aid for Romania, Nicu continued to be active in the work of the Lord. He helped establish seven Romanian churches in Germany and also served in German churches. Today he is still involved in church leadership and pastoral work. Nicu and Monica live in the town of Schwabach, Germany. Their two sons are now married and have given Nicu and Monica five grandchildren.

Many years passed before Nicu told people how he had smuggled Bibles and Christian literature into Romania along with the food parcels. He shares his testimony and special thanks:

> The three years I helped Christian Aid for Romania were a high point in my life. My connection with Christian Aid for Romania was the Lord's plan, 100 percent. The money sent by so many sponsors reached its destination because this work was planned by God. He is the only One who can do all that He plans. My greatest desire was to take as many Bibles into Romania as possible. God was able to do a lot more than what I was thinking. Hundreds of sponsors were able to help the needy—children and old people alike—in that difficult period from 1987 to 1989. Later God did open special doors

for Christian Aid for Romania to work within the country. All these things are recorded in God's book of eternity.

I think God allowed that period of material difficulties in order to open a channel for delivering Bibles into Romania. Many souls found God through the Bibles. Each family that received clothing or a food parcel also received a Bible. Many were surprised to receive help; they thought no one knew them. All of them thanked God for His help. God used angels from Christian Aid for Romania to help His people, and He will one day reward all who worked for Him.

One angel for whom I am especially grateful is my wife, Ana Monica. My experiences in helping people would not have been possible without her dedication and patience during those years. She is a wife whose "price is far above rubies" (Proverbs 31:10).

Pronunciation Key

Ana Monica Bejenaru	(AH nah moh NEE kah behsh shen NAH roh)
Ani	(ah NEE)
Becica	(BEH gee kah)
Beiuş	(bay HOOSH)
Bistriţa	(BEE steest ah)
Brăila	(bruh EE lah)
bunica	(boo NEE kah)
bunicu	(boo NEE koo)
Câmpia	(KUHM pee ah)
Catarina	(kaht ah REEN ah)
Cristian	(KREEST ee ahn)
Constanţa	(kohn STAHN tsah)
Costel	(koh STEHL)
Costică	(koh STEE kuh)
Deva	(DEH vah)
Elena Boghian	(eh LEHN ah Boh GYAHN)
Emanuela	(eh mahn yoo EH lah)
Estera	(ehs TEH rah)
Feri	(FEH ree)
Florin	(FLOH reen)
Galaţi	(gah LAHTZ)
Gheorghe	(GYOHR geh)
Haţeg	(HAHTZ ehg)

Hodoroabă	(hoh doh RAH buh)
Iaşi	(yahsh)
Ieremia	(eh ah MEE ah)
Ilie	(EE lee eh)
Ioan Trif	(Y' WAHN Treef)
Iosif	(YOH seef)
Lidia	(LEE dee ah)
Lili	(LEE lee)
Liviu Olah	(LEE vee oo OH lah)
Marcel	(mahr CHEHL)
Mariana	(mah ree AHN nah)
Marza	(MAH zah)
Matei	(MAH tay)
Nicolae Craiovan	(nee koh LAH eh kry oh VAHN)
Nicu	(NEE koo)
Moldova Nouă	(mohl DOH vah NOH uh)
Octavian	(ohk tah VEE AHN)
Oradea	(oh RAH dee ah)
pace	(PAH cheh)
Pavel	(PAH vehl)
Petre	(PEH treh)
Renata	(REH nah tah)
Reşiţa	(REH sheets ah)
Rodica	(roh DEE kah)
schatz	(stahts)
Sibiu	(see BEE oo)
Silvia Tarniceriu	(SEEL vee ah tuhr nee CHEHR yoo)
Simeria	(see MEH ree ah)
Ştefan	(STEH fahn)
Suceava	(soo CHYAH vah)
tata	(TAH tah)
Timişoara	(tee mee SHWAH rah)
Tinu	(TEE noo)
Vatra Dornei	(VAHT rah DOHR nay)
Yushi	(YOO shee)

Author's Note

As a little girl growing up in the southern lands of Georgia, the country of Romania was not unknown to me. Speakers would occasionally come to church and show slides about the country. I also remember listening to a recording by children from Nathaniel Christian Orphanage in Romania, founded by Christian Aid Ministries. I was fascinated by these foreign songs and memorized all of them by heart—though I had no idea what I was singing!

When the book about Silvia Tarniceriu *(God Knows My Size)* was published, I was nine years old. I remember sitting around my mother's chair many nights with my sisters as Mom read the book to us, chapter by chapter. The story of this Christian girl growing up behind the Iron Curtain made a deep impression on me.

Back then I never dreamed that I would someday have the privilege of writing a book about Romania behind the Iron Curtain. As I listened to Nicu and Monica share their story, I was deeply inspired. They have gone through so much, yet they are living examples of what God is able to do with those who are fully committed to Him.

Elena (Boghian) Marza was also there to help with translation. When I asked Nicu, through Elena, about the prison where he stayed after he escaped from Romania, they discovered that they had both stayed in the cell located under the stairway. Nicu was imprisoned there two years before Elena. (You can read Elena's story in the book *Elena, Strengthened Through Trials,* also published by TGS International.)

We sometimes hear the saying, "Truth is stranger than fiction," and I find this to be true in Nicu's story. Many times he was protected by a divine hand. "God is not limited," Nicu said several times during our interviews, and this was proved over and over again throughout the entire book. As I conclude this writing, I can only echo the psalmist: "Among the gods there is none like unto thee, O Lord; neither are there any works like unto thy works" (Psalm 86:8).

—Diane Yoder

Author's Bio

Diane Yoder hones her story-writing craft in southern Indiana, where she lives with her parents and three of her siblings. A long-time lover of writing, Diane published her first story when she was fourteen years old. Through the encouragement of her friends and family, she pursued her dream of writing books. *God's Secret Agent* is her sixth published book.

Diane is a member of Living Waters Mennonite Church. She delights in the beauty she finds in nature, music, words, and people. Her desire and prayer is that her readers will learn to trust Jesus and receive His love.

If you wish to contact Diane, you may write to her at 10279 West Polk Road, Lexington, Indiana 47138, or at Christian Aid Ministries, P.O. Box 360, Berlin, Ohio 44610. She would be happy to hear from you!

About Christian Aid Ministries

Christian Aid Ministries was founded in 1981 as a nonprofit, tax-exempt 501(c)(3) organization. Its primary purpose is to provide a trustworthy and efficient channel for Amish, Mennonite, and other conservative Anabaptist groups and individuals to minister to physical and spiritual needs around the world. This is in response to the command to ". . . do good unto all men, especially unto them who are of the household of faith" (Galatians 6:10).

Each year, CAM supporters provide 15-20 million pounds of food, clothing, medicines, seeds, Bibles, Bible story books, and other Christian literature for needy people. Most of the aid goes to orphans and Christian families. Supporters' funds also help to clean up and rebuild for natural disaster victims, put up Gospel billboards in the U.S., support several church-planting efforts, operate two medical clinics, and provide resources for needy families to make their own living. CAM's main purposes for providing aid are to help and encourage God's people and bring the Gospel to a lost and dying world.

CAM has staff, warehouses, and distribution networks in Romania, Moldova, Ukraine, Haiti, Nicaragua, Liberia, Israel, and Kenya. Aside from management, supervisory personnel, and bookkeeping operations, volunteers do most of the work at CAM locations. Each year, volunteers at our warehouses, field bases, Disaster Response Services projects, and other locations donate over 200,000 hours of work.

CAM's ultimate purpose is to glorify God and help enlarge His kingdom. ". . . whatsoever ye do, do all to the glory of God" (1 Corinthians 10:31).

The Way to God and Peace

We live in a world contaminated by sin. Sin is anything that goes against God's holy standards. When we do not follow the guidelines that God our Creator gave us, we are guilty of sin. Sin separates us from God, the source of life.

Since the time when the first man and woman, Adam and Eve, sinned in the Garden of Eden, sin has been universal. The Bible says that we all have "sinned and come short of the glory of God" (Romans 3:23). It also says that the natural consequence for that sin is eternal death, or punishment in an eternal hell: "Then when lust hath conceived, it bringeth forth sin: and sin, when it is finished, bringeth forth death" (James 1:15).

But we do not have to suffer eternal death in hell. God provided a sacrifice for our sins through the gift of His only Son, Jesus Christ. "For God so loved the world that he gave his only begotten Son, that whosoever believeth in him should not perish, but have everlasting life" (John 3:16).

A sacrifice is something given to benefit someone else. It costs the giver greatly. Jesus was God's sacrifice. Jesus' death takes away the penalty of sin for all those who accept this sacrifice and truly repent of their sins. To repent of sins means to be truly sorry for and turn away from the things we have done that have violated God's standards (Acts 2:38; 3:19).

Jesus died, but He did not remain dead. After three days, God's Spirit miraculously raised Him to life again. God's Spirit does something similar in us. When we receive Jesus as our sacrifice and repent of our sins, our hearts are changed. We become spiritually alive! We develop new desires and attitudes (2 Corinthians 5:17). We begin to make choices that please God (1 John 3:9). If we do fail and commit sins, we can ask God for forgiveness. "If we confess our sins, he is faithful and just to forgive us our sins, and to cleanse us from all unrighteousness" (1 John 1:9).

Once our hearts have been changed, we want to continue growing spiritually. We will be happy to let Jesus be the Master of our lives and will want to become more like Him. To do this, we must meditate on God's Word and commune with God in prayer. We will testify to others of this change by being baptized and sharing the good news of God's victory over sin and death. Fellowship with a faithful group of believers will strengthen our walk with God (1 John 1:7).